Let Us Hear

STUDIES ON THE SEVEN LETTERS
OF CHRIST IN REVELATION 2-3

Nate Holdridge

CrossLink Publishing

CrossLink Publishing
13395 Voyager Pkwy, Ste 130
Colorado Springs, CO 80921
www.crosslinkpublishing.com

Ordering Information:
Quantity sales. Special discounts are available on quantity purchases by corporations, associations, and others. For details, contact the "Special Sales Department" at the address above.

Let Us Hear/Holdridge —1st ed.

ISBN 978-1-63357-138-9

Library of Congress Control Number: 2018933257

First editon: 10 9 8 7 6 5 4 3 2 1

For my Lord, the One who saves, and the One who gave His church the beautiful letters of Revelation 2–3.

Contents

Preface

For centuries, the church of Jesus Christ has received instruction and edification from the letters His apostles gave us. Paul, Peter, and John, amongst others, left the church teachings, doctrines, and exhortations for life in their writings. But Christ also gave us seven letters directly from His mouth, found in Revelation 2–3. These letters were written to seven specific churches but still speak to every church and every believer today.

When dull and lifeless, the content of these letters helps snap the church back into vitality. When carnal, succumbing to temptation, these letters help empower the church to overcome. When flimsy and unbelieving, these letters help lift the church back into the heights of truth. And when cold or lacking the energy of Christ's Spirit, these letters invite the church back into the fire of His presence. For any and every occasion the church—or an individual believer—finds herself in, these words from Christ provide the needed perspective.

Each letter begins with Christ's depiction of Himself, for His description is their prescription. We always need more of our Lord, and these letters help us feast on and with Him.

Each letter from Christ ends by urging the reader to hear what the Spirit has said to the churches. For this reason, great care should be taken when considering these letters. We ought to cry out to the living God and ask for His aid in understanding and applying His words to us. As you sit down to read each chapter, pause to ask for the Father's strength and help in your reading. We certainly need His Spirit to help us open our hearts to His desires, His thoughts, and His corrections.

As a pastor-teacher, I have endeavored to faithfully preach and write about these letters, partly because I have felt their impact. My soul has been warmed and corrected, calmed and strengthened, through these words from our Lord. My hopes and prayers are the same for you, that Christ would dwell richly within you as you ponder His words for your heart.

CHAPTER 1

The Author

Years ago, for a season, I habitually checked the family mailbox—nonstop. My devotion was religious. I had applied to various colleges and awaited their replies, but I did not wait well at all. I was incessant. Multiple times each day I would venture out to the curb, hoping for the letter that would seal my destiny. The wait took longer than I expected. Day after day, catalogs and bills grated on my mind and mission. It seemed the letters I hoped for would never come.

The sender helps us determine the value of the communication. If the sender is a university we are waiting on, someone we admire, or a company we've placed an order with, the correspondence is deemed valuable. If the sender is an advertiser or a utility wanting a payment from us, the correspondence is deemed less desirable.

The same holds true for the seven letters from Christ in Revelation 2–3. There, Jesus spoke to seven different churches in Asia Minor. Each church existed near the end of John's life, which was also the end of the first century. Each letter ends with the phrase, "He who has an ear, let him hear what the Spirit says to the churches." To have an ear to hear, they needed to appreciate the sender.

This is true for us as well. The seven letters overflow with powerful exhortations from Christ—words of warning, comfort, and promise. But we will think little of them if we don't have a vision for the magnificence of the sender. A low view of Christ will create an apathetic glossing over of these seven letters. A high view of Christ will create an urgency and anticipation as we pore over these seven letters. If we see Jesus, if we know of His transcendent position, we will read these letters with rapt attention.

This is why it is important to begin a book on the seven letters with the vision John has of Christ in Revelation 1. To hear Jesus well, we must see Jesus well—and see him John does. John had, of course, seen Jesus throughout three years of friendship and work here on earth. How he sees Christ in Revelation 1 is altogether different. He had known Jesus in His humbled humanity, but this is a vision of Him in His glorified state—a mixture of humanity and divinity. John attempts, by the aid of the Holy Spirit, to write about it. This vision of Christ helps us prepare to read the letters from Christ.

The Apostle

> I, John, your brother and partner in the tribulation and the kingdom and the patient endurance that are in Jesus, was on the island called Patmos on account of the word of God and the testimony of Jesus. (Revelation 1:9)

John was an incredible man with an incredible life story. Peter or Paul he was not. God had a different plan for his life. Paul had traveled and written profusely. Peter had led and taught courageously. John had endured and exhorted lovingly. He is nearing the end of his race when he receives the final book of the Bible—the Revelation of Jesus Christ.

John receives this letter while on the island of Patmos, which was used as a Roman prison. He is there for preaching the Word of God and testifying about Jesus Christ. In short, he is imprisoned for proclaiming the gospel. The details aren't given by John, for this isn't the Revelation of John, but of Christ. Still, we marvel that a man so obedient to Christ would suffer as John did. Here he is, an old man near the close of the first century. Retirement and ease are not his, but a suffering for the cause of Christ is.

We ought to think of John when we're thirsty for great revelation from God. We might be tempted to crave God's opening of our hearts and minds, but only in places of comfort. For John, and for so many before and after him, revelation was attached to pain. In that state of suffering, God has often been allowed to perform His finest work. This isn't a requirement; we don't need to hunt for pain. But if and when it comes our way, it might allow Jesus Christ a chance for His deepest work in our lives.

The Letters

> I was in the Spirit on the Lord's day, and I heard behind me a loud voice like a trumpet saying, "Write what you see in a book and send it to the seven churches, to Ephesus and to Smyrna and to Pergamum and to Thyatira and to Sardis and to Philadelphia and to Laodicea." (Revelation 1:10–11)

There, suffering on Patmos, John is caught up in the Spirit on the Lord's day (Revelation 1:10). Likely, John means that on a Sunday, he is given the entire miraculous vision of the book of

Revelation by the Holy Spirit. The initial contact he receives comes in the form of a loud voice like a trumpet. This is the voice of Christ telling him to write what he sees in a book and send it to the seven churches.

Ephesus, Smyrna, Pergamum, Thyatira, Sardis, Philadelphia, and Laodicea were all cities in Asia Minor, the western coastal region of modern-day Turkey. Starting with Ephesus, traveling north to Pergamum, then southeast down to Laodicea, the seven cities formed a bit of a circuit. The route of these letters loosely forms a capital A.

The letters Jesus authored are orderly and consistent. For all the differences between them in content, they contain many similarities. One significant similarity is that each letter begins with an autobiographical description of Jesus. This seems very intentional. Each church needed refreshment in some aspect of Christ's nature and personality, and addressing their deficiencies in this way shows us that the answer is always Jesus. For instance, the church in Smyrna was the persecuted and suffering church. For them, it was encouraging to know of Jesus as the One "who died and came to life" (Revelation 2:8). This reminder of Jesus's resurrection would have filled the church in Smyrna with hope for their own future resurrection.

Another similarity in the letters is that most of them contain a compliment from Jesus—something He admires about each church. Only the letter to the church in Laodicea lacks any complimentary word from Christ. Every other church—even those steeped in some form of sin or doctrinal error—receives at least a small word of commendation. Through these affirmations, the modern reader can learn about the value system of Christ.

Additionally, five of the letters include a word of correction regarding something that needs changing in their relationship to Christ; only two churches receive no such exhortation. As the church, we are God's children, and as the Father, He instructs and even disciplines us. Just as we are to hear His voice, these original churches were no different. They needed to receive the word of Christ . . . even the corrective word of Christ.

Note also, every letter ends with a promise from Christ to the overcomer. These promises are unique and, at first glance, odd to the modern reader. Christ promises mysterious things like hidden manna, a white stone, and the morning star. He also offers more definable things like the tree of life, white garments, and a name written in the book of life. These promises are eternal in nature but also designed for the issues found within each of the seven churches.

Finally, near the end of every letter is this phrase: "He who has an ear, let him hear what the Spirit says to the churches" (Revelation 2:7, 11, 17, 29; 3:6, 13, 22). Again, this phrase serves as an exhortation to receive the word of Christ. It shows there is a real possibility a church might resist His word. Atrocities were found in some of these churches. They should resist His word no longer. They needed to hear. This final statement stands as a word of encouragement—listen! But it is also a warning—you might not listen!

It seems important to note the historical reality of these seven churches. All seven existed in John's day. Across the horizon, from Patmos, he could see them in his mind's eye. He knew these churches. Christ had selected these seven because they were real churches with real issues. Why, for instance, Jesus chose not to write to the church in Colossae, located very near the church in

Laodicea, is unknown. It was His sovereign choice to write to these seven, for they were actual churches in actual need.

Additionally, these seven churches all seem to be in existence today. A local church or denomination might find alignment with the coldness of Ephesus or the little strength of Philadelphia. They might connect to the lukewarmness of Laodicea or the apostasy of Thyatira. Some churches will identify closely with the persecution endured by Smyrna. Others will connect to the deadness in Sardis.

But the attitudes of these churches likely exist within every local church as well. While the overarching mood of a congregation might be that of Laodicea, for instance, there will be some members who carry the Philadelphian heart within them. If a local congregation has a broad reach, then it is possible that there are elements of all seven churches found within it. Again, one of the letters might most closely align with a church overall while the individual believers within that church will connect with all seven letters.

Furthermore, all seven letters and churches likely exist within the heart of every believer. I have found elements of every church in my own heart. Sometimes the Ephesian coldness and the Philadelphian love battle within me. Other times the Pergamum license and the Smyrna purity are at war. It is possible for individual believers to go the route of any of these churches. Sometimes this manifests itself in seasons of life, when we live and think more like one of the seven for a time and then shift to another as the years go by. At other times the attitudes of all seven churches simultaneously jockey for position.

So these letters are of extreme value to the modern church and every modern believer. We ought to read them with close attention to what the Spirit might say to us today. To that end, it is valuable for us to consider the author of these letters. We've considered the scribe—John—but we must also consider the originator. To hear His letters well, we must see His attributes well.

The Author

> Then I turned to see the voice that was speaking to me, and on turning I saw seven golden lampstands, and in the midst of the lampstands one like a son of man, clothed with a long robe and with a golden sash around his chest. The hairs of his head were white, like white wool, like snow. His eyes were like a flame of fire, his feet were like burnished bronze, refined in a furnace, and his voice was like the roar of many waters. In his right hand he held seven stars, from his mouth came a sharp two-edged sword, and his face was like the sun shining in full strength. (Revelation 1:12–16)

It is at this point John "turned to see the voice that was speaking" (Revelation 1:12). John is not content with mere information; he wants to see the One speaking to Him. This personal turning is all-important—especially for John (and us), as the great Revelation occurs after it. What—and initially who—John saw amazes him.

> The first things John sees are seven golden lampstands. Interestingly, these lampstands are seemingly singular in nature. They weren't connected like the menorah of the Jewish temple. Later, Jesus will tell the church of Ephesus that He will remove their lampstand if they do not repent. Again, this removability seems to indicate seven individual lampstands (candlesticks).

Fortunately for the reader, Jesus gives a clear interpre-
tation of them. They are the seven churches (Revelation 1:20).

In the midst of those lampstands, John sees "one like a son of
man" (Revelation 1:12). This title—"son of man"—was Jesus's fa-
vorite title for Himself, having used it over eighty times in the
gospel accounts. The title originated in the Old Testament. It is
found in Ezekiel 2:1, where God addresses the prophet Ezekiel as
"Son of man." This is also the same title Daniel uses when he saw
Jesus in a vision and describes Him "like a son of man" (Daniel
7:13).

John is seeing the glorified Christ. John had known the Son of
Man in His earthly ministry and had watched Him ascend back
to heaven. But He had not yet seen the exalted Christ. This is
the seventeenth post-resurrection appearance of Christ, and
John recognizes his Lord. Having been close to Christ when He
walked the earth, John knows what He looks like. And after all,
he was the disciple "whom Jesus loved" (John 13:23). He was so
close to Jesus, he was found leaning on Him during the Last Sup-
per. So here, John sees Jesus in His glorified state and writes that
he sees one "like" the Son of Man. Jesus looks very different to
John, but He can still see the resemblance. The One he'd walked
with in Galilee is now standing before him eternally, and he gives
us a vivid description of what he sees.

Working

So John sees the glorified Christ in the midst of the lampstands,
and the first detail he records about Christ concerns his clothing.
Jesus wears a long robe and has a golden sash around his chest,
and later in Revelation we will see others coming out of the sanc-
tuary of God wearing similar garments.

One of the duties of the Old Testament priests was tending to the lampstands within the tabernacle. They maintained them by cleaning off the soot, refilling the oil, and trimming the wicks. Their inspections and regular maintenance were designed to keep the fires burning brightly. Here, John sees the heavenly temple and finds Jesus, our Great High Priest, working hard to make the fires of these churches burn brightly. The church is to shine, for we are the light of the world—extensions of Christ, who is the true light of the world (Matthew 5:14, John 1:9). John sees Jesus working on the churches, tending to them and their needs.

Jesus is working on His church! He had told Peter (and the others), "I will build my church" (Matthew 16:18). He is the One who, after ascending, by the Spirit gave spiritual gifts. He also gave spiritual offices—apostles, prophets, evangelists, pastors, and teachers to equip the saints for the work of ministry (Ephesians 4:8–12). The seven churches needed this vision. They needed to see the current work of Christ in heaven—trimming and cleaning and refilling, all in an attempt to see them shine brightly.

Jesus has a more excellent ministry right now (Hebrews 8:6). He is writing His law onto our minds and hearts (Hebrews 8:10), changing us and our perspectives from the inside out. This is His continual New Covenant work in us (2 Corinthians 3:18). He is working.

The Lord has not left His people alone. Christ is not vacationing until His bodily and visible return. No, He is maintaining His church, building it over the years. Every local church should ask: What does Jesus Christ want to work in us? Every believer should ask: What does Jesus Christ want to work in me? Jesus never slumbers nor sleeps (Psalm 121:3–4), and He lives to make intercession for us (Hebrews 7:25). At His ascension, He began a new work. What will He work in you?

Wise

John next sees Jesus's hair. It is white . . . white as wool, like snow. This detail is fascinating, for it's found in the everyday human experience. We'll never meet people who have eyes like a flame of fire, but we will meet those with white hair. In the Bible, as in our modern times, white hair indicates age, which also indicates experience.

But Jesus's hair is not naturally grayed from a long life. This is Christ in His glorified state, not as an old man, yet His hair is pure white here. This type of purity is indicated by John's double description—it is white like wool and snow. The Bible uses this type of language to describe moral purity . . . sinlessness . . . a cleanness before God. Here, God the Son is seen with pure white hair.

All of this taken together points us to the experience and purity of Christ. On earth, we ought to look to those who have gone before us. The older generations are to serve as teachers for the younger generations. Jesus is the ultimate example in this. His experience is without equal, and His wisdom is of the purest variety. No man or woman could ever claim wisdom equal to His. It is paramount.

Jesus Christ, the eternal Son of God, has seen the rise of every civilization, no matter how small, in all of human history. Every civilization that has fallen, Christ has seen. He has seen the individual souls—the thoughts and impulses and motivations—of every person inside those civilizations. He has watched every war, every conflict, every famine, every decision. Nothing has escaped His vision.

Jesus has seen every relationship that has ever existed. He knows the thoughts and feelings of every person within those relationships. He has seen every marriage, every divorce, and every family. He's observed loneliness and fatigue, conflict and strife. He has seen it all.

Near the beginning of His public ministry, at a Passover feast in Jerusalem, His fame began to grow as a result of the signs He performed. People began to believe in His name, although it was a superficial belief based on the miraculous (John 2:23). Jesus would not commit Himself to them, "because he knew all people . . . for he himself knew what was in man" (John 2:24–25). He knew man. He knew what was in man.

All this points to the extreme experience and wisdom of Jesus Christ, the Son of Man, the Son of God. He has wisdom of the eternal variety. It is pure and good and right and true. We often run to friends or family or culture for our wisdom, but Christ's wisdom is eternal. It is lasting and true. He is the ultimate mentor, the final Word, the true light.

In preparation to receive these letters, the seven churches should have fixed their gaze on His wisdom. If we believe He has this pure, experienced wisdom for us, will we act as if it is so? Will we long for His letters with anticipation? Will we turn to see the voice that speaks with us?

All-Seeing

Now John points out that Jesus has eyes like a flame of fire. Robes and sashes and even white hair are not yet strange visions, but this attribute helps us see the magnificence of the vision. Christ had eyes like fire. One instinctively looks into the eyes of a man or beast, and John instinctively looks into the eyes of His Lord. He must have been overwhelmed at the sight.

It is important to note that the church in Thyatira received this description of Christ. They were, as we will see, a deceived church in need of correction. They were living outside His will for their church. They'd received poisonous doctrines and teachings into their fellowship. Understanding this helps us understand the impact of John's vision of Jesus. The eyes of fire might indicate the all-seeing eyes of Jesus. In His exalted and glorified position, He sees everything in His church. Nothing escapes His attention.

This, of course, can serve as a word of great comfort. Pregnant and alone in the wilderness, a young Hagar discovers the Lord as The-God-Who-Sees (Genesis 16:13). She has not escaped His sight, and her prayers have not escaped His ear. It is comforting to the modern believer to know that we cannot escape the wonderful sight of God. The Lord looks upon us; He sees our plight. With the psalmist, we say, "In God, whose word I praise, in God I trust; I shall not be afraid. What can flesh do to me?" (Psalm 56:4).

However, Thyatira should not have received this description of Christ as a word of comfort, but of warning. He saw everything in their midst. Nothing was hidden from His sight; He saw everything within and about them. A recognition of this was needed in the Thyatira church.

The vision of Christ is total, in the sense that He sees all. But His vision is also perfect, in the sense that He interprets all He sees with precise accuracy. His vision cut through every motivation of the Thyatira church (as we shall see when studying that letter), and His vision cuts through us. He knows me better than I know myself. He sees right through me, and my every thought or motivation is well-known to Him.

This carries with it the possibility either of fright or hope for the believer. If we misunderstand His grace and mercy, His perfect vision of every detail in us might cause us to be overwhelmed with guilt. If He sees all, how might we ever measure up? If no sin is secret from Him, how could we ever be right with and by Him? But the believer who sees the cross well understands that the all-penetrating sight of Christ has hope embedded within it. He sees our sin, yet He loves us and calls us to repent and turn to Him. His eyes of fire are eyes of grace, for grace is not ignorant of or a redefiner of sin. Grace does not erase His holiness but is necessary because of it.

We would do well to remember His sight. Let us not toil in disobedience or secret sin, thinking we have fooled anyone. We have not fooled Him . . . yet there He is, graciously drawing us back to Himself.

Judge

The feet of Christ next draw John's attention. They are like burnished bronze that has been refined in a furnace. His feet (and possibly his legs) remind John of pure bronze. Perhaps the intimidating eyes of fire cause John to look away and down at the feet of Christ. Bronze is often the metal of judgment in Scripture, and this bronze is burnished and refined. It is of the purest and strongest variety.

These pure feet seem indicative of something strong, for the church in Thyatira also received this description of Christ. They were a church that had made various judgments and doctrinal statements—but in error. They needed a prescription for this sickness within them, and the bronze feet of Christ were their good medicine. This seems to mean they needed the pure and lasting and strong and true judgment of Christ to replace their human opinions.

The judgments of Christ are eternal facts, not temporary opinions. The church often feels pressure to conform its views to society's, but the judgments of Christ are what matters. Cultures will "know God's righteous decree" regarding sinful activities but will "not only do them but give approval to those who practice them" (Romans 1:32). But in the end, we will not care at all about the opinion of mankind; only of the opinion of God will matter.

Believers do well to see Christ and His eternal, pure, and lasting judgments. We must work hard to make certain we have discerned His judgments from His Word, because too much of what the church has stood for is mere tradition, human invention, and legalism. But His Word is worth standing up for and believing in. Believers operate by a new set of rules and judgments, which aren't actually new or old, but eternal, for God has designed them.

Perhaps the glorified Christ has a judgment to offer you. Perhaps He has a perspective that grates against your sensibilities. Perhaps the culture has so discipled and trained you that His Word and judgments are hard to handle. Let these letters and His nature wash over you and your discomfort.

Speaking

The next part of John's vision has little to do with sight but instead focuses on sound. He hears the voice of Christ, and it is like the roar of many waters. His voice is loud and crushing and beautiful, like an immense waterfall. No single church received this description—I think because all churches need it. His Word is vital to our lives.

His Word, like the roar of many waters, is to become so loud to us that we cannot hear anything else. I do not mean to say we should never read or listen to or learn anything other than Bible verses. What I mean is that His Word should become so strong to us that we are not easily swayed from Scripture. When the voice of Christ is louder than all other voices, we grow, and our joy maximizes.

His Word, like the roar of many waters, is the collection of various streams and rivers into one. Moses and David and Daniel and Matthew all converge into one rushing river that is the voice of Christ. It is about Him, and it is from Him. He is the author. He is the subject. The totality of the Bible, with all its various human authors and settings, has come together as the powerful voice of Christ. Eternally, this voice will sing to His people, overwhelming us with its sheer power.

His Word, like the roar of many waters, is constant in nature. He is never silent, for the Bible has been written and is available to all. Jesus Christ, in this facet of His description by John, should be seen as speaking to His church. His Word is constant and steady, readily available. We need not go outside it. We need not neglect it. We need not think we have mastered it. No, we ought to listen to it in its constant flow.

> Blessed is the man who walks not in the counsel of the wicked, nor stands in the way of sinners, nor sits in the seat of scoffers; but his delight is in the law of the Lord, and on his law he meditates day and night. He is like a tree planted by streams of water that yields its fruit in

its season, and its leaf does not wither. In all that he
does, he prospers. (Psalm 1:1–3)

If we allow the powerful Word of the glorified Christ to flow into
us, it will fascinate and teach us for all eternity.

Holding

John sees the right hand of Christ, and in it are seven stars. Later
in the passage, we discover the identity of these seven stars—
they are the angels of the seven churches (Revelation 1:20). Each
time Jesus begins a letter to a church, He starts by saying, "To the
angel of the church of. . ." Every church had an angel, and here
Jesus is holding those angels in His right hand.

This raises a question: What does it mean that each church had
an angel? This is not a repeated concept throughout the New
Testament—that churches have an individual angelic being over
them. There are some hints at regional or national angels in Daniel's writings (Daniel 10:13, 20; 12:1). Personal angels are alluded
to in the New Testament narratives (Matthew 18:10, Acts 12:15).
But this is not a fully developed concept with sharp understand-
ings of how this angelic realm works.

Some have taken the pure meaning of the word angel and applied
it to the pastors in each church. Strictly speaking, angel means
"messenger." So even though this word is only used in reference
to the angelic realm in the New Testament, some have thought
Jesus is breaking that practice here. Some have thought Jesus is
referring instead to human messengers. Although there is room
for this possibility, this might be straining the text.

I take these angels as some form of spiritual leadership within
the churches. Whether angelic (part of the unseen realm) or human (part of the visible realm), the role of Christ is clear: He

holds them in His right hand. This speaks of His firm grip on the leadership of the churches. He holds the influencers of these churches in His hand.

This teaches us of the security of Christ. In His current glorified state, He works to hold the leaders securely. He is in control. He has a firm grip on His church and His people.

> My sheep hear my voice, and I know them, and they follow me. I give them eternal life, and they will never perish, and no one will snatch them out of my hand. My Father, who has given them to me, is greater than all, and no one is able to snatch them out of the Father's hand. I and the Father are one. (John 10:27–30)

Discipline

John observes a sharp, two-edged sword coming from the mouth of Christ. This might remind the New Testament reader of the Hebrews concept that "the word of God is living and active, sharper than any two-edged sword" (Hebrews 4:12). Additionally, we are reminded of the spiritual armor of Ephesians and that the "sword of the Spirit" is the "word of God" (Ephesians 6:17).

These are striking parallels to John's vision of the exalted Christ. His Word is a treasure to the church, able to cut into the core of our being. His Word is a weapon for the Spirit, a primary tool for advancing God's kingdom. Still, this might not hold the fullest meaning of the sword here. John is describing a heavy sword, the kind used by Roman soldiers to kill and destroy. It is this same sword that is used in victorious judgment at the return of Christ (Revelation 19:15). In other words, this particular sword seems to have more than a bit of discipline and judgment attached to it.

One major evidence for the sword taking a more corrective tone is the fact that the church in Pergamum received this description of Christ. They were wayward and needed the discipline of Christ in their fellowship. So perhaps it is best to see this sword as the powerful Word of Christ, a Word that performs the needed task, which is sometimes discipline.

God is a good Father who disciplines His children. He does not leave us alone but interacts with our lives. He changes us and works to grow us. "He disciplines us for our good, that we may share his holiness" (Hebrews 12:10).

The question is, will we receive His disciplinary word in our lives? Will we allow ourselves to come under the corrective word of Christ? Again, in preparation for these letters, the answer must be in the affirmative. The letters are not entirely corrective, for Christ will speak praises and promises in them. But they do contain some words of correction. If we are prone to stiffen when His Word interacts with us in a more corrective way, we will miss out on the blessings attached to these words.

Majestic

Finally, John sees the face of Christ, and it is like the sun shining in full strength (Revelation 1:16). This is the glory of God in the face of Christ. John is observing divinity.

There was a moment in the life of Christ when He took Peter, James, and our human author, John, up to a mountaintop for prayer. They fell asleep, but He became transfigured before them. His deity peeked out. They awoke to see His face shining like the sun and His garments whitened like no launderer on earth could whiten them (Matthew 17:2). This was a glimpse into Christ's eternal glory. Here, John sees that glory permanently affixed to Christ.

This glory radiates from the face of Christ and is meant to impact the church, His people. He lives within all true believers, so now the mystery is revealed, "which is Christ in you, the hope of glory" (Colossians 1:27). The glory of Christ is meant to change us, for as we interact with Him, we are all "being transformed into the same image" (2 Corinthians 3:18).

His shining face is meant to show us the wonder and majesty of the One we worship. This is the real, glorified Jesus. No matter who we construct in our minds, Jesus is majestically awesome. Whereas "we once regarded Christ according to the flesh, we regard him thus no longer" (2 Corinthians 5:16).

Do you want to know Him? Do you long to hear His beautiful voice as He speaks to His church? Let the Spirit give you ears to hear as we journey through each letter to each of His churches. He stands, speaking, but we must emulate John's example. He turns to see the voice, so we must turn to see as well. He has spoken, and that voice still resounds today. He wants His church to turn and see the One who is speaking to them.

CHAPTER 2

Ephesus

Anyone who's married will tell you the goal is quantity with quality. To have a long and enduring marriage lacking in love and joy is painful. Congratulations are in order for keeping your word, the covenant of your youth, but the goal is to have more than length of years. We want gladness within the marriage.

I recently spoke with a woman I respect who has enjoyed sixty-two years of marriage to her husband. Amazing! Celebrating numbers like these is wonderful. Ten-, twenty-five-, and fifty-year marriages are worthy of praise. They have stood and kept the covenants of their youth.

Still, for all the length, we long for love. For all the quantity, we long for quality. No one envisions a long and lasting marriage filled with bitterness and heartache. That isn't the goal. No, we long for long marriages that are long on love. We want a quality of love to join the quantity of years.

This strikes at the idea of Christ's letter to the church in Ephesus. As we will see, their quantity was immense, but they had begun to lack in quality. They had done much for Christ yet were far from Him at this moment in their existence. It was time to revisit their first love, so Christ wrote to them.

Description of Ephesus

The city of Ephesus was a great city of the Roman Empire. Located in Asia Minor, Ephesus was the premier city of that region. All of the other churches and cities we will look at in this book owed a debt of gratitude to this city and the church within it.

Commercially great. With three major Roman highways converging within it, plus a seacoast facing Rome on its edge, Ephesus had become a place of wealth and trade. Opulence ruled the day. Its prosperity was visible, and so were its vices. The church in Ephesus had to battle this.

Politically great. Ephesus was considered a free city, complete with its own Senate. The de facto capital of that region, Roman governors resided there. Self-governed and free, Ephesus stood as a jewel of the empire.

Religiously great. The people of Ephesus were famous for their worship of the fertility god Diana (or Artemis to the Greeks). Their temple to her was one of the wonders of the ancient world. Thousands of priest and priestesses were employed in her service, many through cult prostitution. This was abhorrent to God, of course, but famous among mankind.

This was the city the church found itself in. Our modern minds might believe it was easier to live a Christian life during biblical times. The way current culture and society views followers of Christ is that we are "odd." While we might think this is a new view of the Christian life, one look at cities like Ephesus and Corinth and Rome and even Jerusalem ought to erase that from our minds. Christians in every generation and location have experienced challenges. The church in Ephesus was no different. They were forced to stand out for their faithful service to Christ.

But for all we know of the city of Ephesus, we know much more about the church in Ephesus. They were a great church with a great history, the kind of church we would be proud to be a part of. Their fruit and labor were astoundingly powerful; Christ had used them to the fullest degree.

The church got its start during Paul's second missionary journey. After a season of service in Corinth, Paul had traveled briefly to Ephesus, only to depart rather quickly for Macedonia. Still, this first foray meant Paul would drop off his married friends Priscilla and Aquila in Ephesus, a simple act God used beautifully. It seems there was a powerful preacher in Ephesus named Apollos. He was a skilled orator, readily familiar with the Old Testament. Still, all he had exposure to was the baptism of John. He had heard of Jesus but not of His atoning work—the redemption of the cross—so it was absent from his message.

This is where Priscilla and Aquila were able to help. They knew the gospel message, so they politely taught Apollos the full gospel. The man believed and became a powerful gospel preacher and Bible teacher. However most of his gospel ministry did not occur in Ephesus but in Corinth, for he departed from Ephesus after becoming a believer.

Paul returned to Ephesus after Apollos departed. He found the remnant of Apollos's previous ministry in the form of some disciples, "about twelve men in all" (Acts 19:7). Upon meeting them, Paul ascertained they had not yet received the Spirit. They had only been baptized into John the Baptist's baptism. Like Apollos, they had not yet heard the gospel message. Paul preached it to them, and the rest is history. After three months of synagogue evangelism, Paul began teaching these young disciples every day in a rented school. He did this for two years. As a result, "all the residents of Asia heard the word of the Lord, both Jews and Greeks" (Acts 19:10).

It seems Paul discovered a powerful ministry style there in Ephesus. He taught; they were equipped. They—not he—went out into all of Asia Minor sharing the word of the Lord. He seems to allude to this pattern of ministry in Ephesians 4: "And he gave the apostles, the prophets, the evangelists, the shepherds and teachers, to equip the saints for the work of ministry, for building up the body of Christ" (Ephesians 4:11–12). Again, he taught; they were equipped.

After this fruitful season of ministry, a rebellion against Paul and the gospel he preached rose up in Ephesus. Instigated by those who crafted and sold idols for the goddess Diana, Paul was driven out of town. Paul later visited the elders of the Ephesian church on the island of Miletus. He was on his way to Jerusalem, but on that island Paul poured out a powerful message to the leaders of the church in Ephesus. It was a message pastors and leaders in every generation have gleaned much from.

Many believe John became the pastor of the church in Ephesus at this time. Later, as Paul alluded to in his letters to Timothy, Timothy became its pastor (see 1 Timothy 1:3, 2 Timothy 4:12).

The conclusion of this brief history of the church in Ephesus is that they'd been a wonderfully fruitful church with ministry zeal and focus. They had worked well and hard for Christ, going out into all the region with the gospel message. Their great heritage had equipped them for a great work of ministry. Now, thirty-five years later, Jesus writes to this same church.

Description of Jesus

> To the angel of the church in Ephesus write: "The
> words of him who holds the seven stars in his right
> hand, who walks among the seven golden lampstands."
> (Revelation 2:1)

Christ's self-description refers back to John's vision of the seven
stars and seven golden lampstands (Revelation 1:12, 20). There,
Jesus told John the stars were the angels (or leaders) and the
lampstands were the churches. So Christ is seen, in Ephesus,
holding the leaders and the churches in His right hand. He holds
the angels. He holds the churches.

The Ephesian believers needed to know of this nearness of Christ.
Though their love for Him was waning, His love for them was
not. His love was strong and vibrant. Though they had left their
early fervency for Christ, He had remained fervent for them.
This letter stands as a plea for them to return to their former love
and devotion.

Praise

> I know your works, your toil and your patient endur-
> ance, and how you cannot bear with those who are evil,
> but have tested those who call themselves apostles and
> are not, and found them to be false. I know you are
> enduring patiently and bearing up for my name's sake,
> and you have not grown weary. . . . This you have: you
> hate the works of the Nicolaitans, which I also hate.
> (Revelation 2:2–3, 6)

In between many words of praise for the Ephesian church, Jesus had one simple word of correction. The praise is not mere

flattery, for Christ is incapable of that. No, these are the generous words of admiration from Christ for His church. They are attributes He values, and since He values them, we value them.

He praises them for their works, saying, "I know your works, your toil and your patient endurance" (Revelation 2:2). They were a working church—so much so, in fact, that their work had turned into toil and necessitated patient endurance. Work is one thing, but toil and the need for patience are another. This was work of the sacrificial variety. They were not a social club or a collection of friends; rather, they were hardworking Christians on a mission for Jesus Christ.

This is noteworthy praise. When the man Araunah offered to give Israel's King David his threshing floor as a place for sacrifice, David replied he would pay full price. He did not want to "offer burnt offerings to the Lord my God that cost me nothing" (2 Samuel 24:24). David's was a costly worship. He knew it needed to be so, and the church in Ephesus worked in like spirit. They endured patiently and did not grow weary (Revelation 2:3).

Additionally, Jesus praises them for their carefulness in doctrine and teaching. Perhaps due to the good start they'd had from Paul's teaching ministry, the Ephesian church did not bear with those who were evil. They tested and rejected false apostles (Revelation 2:2). They didn't believe everything they heard and were able to test new winds of doctrine against the right doctrine of God's Word. Astute to the core, the Ephesian church was careful when confronted with new ideas and movements. They weren't skeptical for skepticism's sake, for that is easy. Instead, they were able to test doctrines because they were already biblically alert.

This alertness led to a rejection of the works of the Nicolaitans, something Jesus also praises them for (2:6). The Nicolaitan doctrine was probably of the antinomian variety. It turned God's grace into license. Whatever this doctrine was, the Pergamum church embraced it. We might not know exactly what this doctrine was, but we do know Pergamum had already adopted a loose sex ethic. This makes it likely the Nicolaitan error had encouraged them in their license. Ephesus, however, was not so easily deceived. Jesus commends this church for their readiness with and in the Word of God.

Taking all of Jesus's words of commendation as is, the reader comes away believing the church in Ephesus was a great church. They didn't only have a great history but also a current fruitfulness unto Christ. If we had lived in that day, we might call this the most magnificent church we had ever seen. They had been explosive with the gospel—a dynamic center of gospel preaching and faithful Bible teaching. Jesus thought highly of this church, not only in the past but in their present.

Correction

> But I have this against you, that you have abandoned
> the love you had at first. (Revelation 2:4)

For all His words of praise, Christ has a word of correction as well. It is a strong word. As the Lord of His people, as the husband of His bride, as the Chief Shepherd of the flock, as the real senior pastor of the ecclesia, Christ speaks. "But I have this against you," Jesus says.

Before considering the correction itself, consider the act of correction from the Lord. Does not His deep and pure love mandate His saying, "But I have this against you"? Would it be loving if He kept these corrections to Himself? Not at all. It is the deepest and holiest of loves that forces Jesus to speak. He cannot sit idly by and watch this church self-destruct. He sees something in them akin to cancer. No good physician would give a patient temporary happiness by refusing to disclose cancer in them. No, that temporary happiness would only lead to long-term pain. The cancer would remain untreated, dominating the body. So it is with Christ. He sees the cancer and must deal with it.

We understand this action instinctively. Parents crave the happiness of their children, but parents (mostly) know a difference exists between happiness now and happiness later. If I teach my children to work hard, it leads to happiness later—sometimes at the cost of their happiness now. I could make them happy now by cultivating laziness in them, but this would lead to pain later. Parents see this in a thousand contexts—happiness now often leads to pain later. Jesus, like a good parent, is willing to tell the Ephesians and the Thyatirans and the Laodiceans (and us) the truth. If it hurts now, it can lead to joy later. This is love.

To the Ephesians, there was only one thing in need of attention. "I have this against you, that you have abandoned the love you had at first" (Revelation 2:4). For all the work of the Ephesian church, they lacked love—at least "first love" love. They were fruitful for Christ, but the inner motivation of the heart was off kilter. Their love was lacking. They had, in the words of Christ, abandoned it. They had left their first love.

But what does it mean for them to have abandoned their first love? Is this an emotional love? Were they to go back to all the initial passions of the former days? What was Christ longing for? What was the love they had at the first?

"First love," it seems, is marital love. Spouses in a strong marriage will grow closer in their oneness, deeper in their love, and fuller in the knowledge of each other. In the same manner, the church in Ephesus has grown in their marital love to Christ, but they have drifted.

To the Corinthian church, Paul had said, "I betrothed you to one husband, to present you as a pure virgin to Christ. But I am afraid that as the serpent deceived Eve by his cunning, your thoughts will be led astray from a sincere and pure devotion to Christ" (2 Corinthians 11:2–3). For the Corinthians, Paul worried they would be swayed from a "sincere and pure devotion to Christ." He had betrothed them to Christ, and he wanted them to persist in a simple and undistracted devotion to Him.

But this is the threat to our marital love with Jesus. We love to add complexity to it all. "Of making many books there is no end" (Ecclesiastes 12:12), and with our many books, we can muddy the waters of simple devotion to Christ. Our principles for peace get in the way of the Prince of peace. Our programs distract us from His program. Our ministry to the world makes us forget His ministry to us. As the years tick by, we might love what we can produce for Christ more than Christ Himself. Our sanctification becomes more loved than the Sanctifier. The fruit becomes more lovely than the One the fruit is for.

This marital love is not honeymoon love. What I mean to say is that the love is to deepen. Honeymoon love is good, but it is yet undeveloped and is shallow in comparison to the deeper love possible after years of strong marriage. The jolts of nervous excitement that come upon a new couple will fade, giving way to a deeper knowledge and appreciation for each other. On the wedding day, God proclaims, "The two have become one." As marital love deepens, oneness becomes less of a position believed and more of an experience lived. The church in Ephesus was not to go back to an immature love but to deepen in a mature, marital love with Jesus.

Marital love is response love. "We love because He first loved us," John wrote, and this is true (1 John 4:19). Was it not to the Ephesians Paul wrote to of the mystery of marriage—that it is a representation of the relationship between Christ and His church? "This mystery is profound," he wrote, "and I am saying that it refers to Christ and the church" (Ephesians 5:32). Jesus's love for His church is entirely unselfish, for He thinks not of Himself. His cross was the ultimate in selfless sacrifice for a bride, and that same heart is His today. Our love is a response to that selfless love of Christ.

But the church in Ephesus had ceased to do all their works in the light of the great love of Christ for them. They did them because they were good. They did them because they were right. They did them because they were of great value. They did them because they had the truth. They did them for a thousand reasons, but the love of Christ had ceased to be the driving force. Christ saw them, and from His glorified position, He pointed out their error. "You have abandoned the love you had at first."

So first love is response love. And Jesus Christ is looking for this marital response kind of love. He longs for it. He wants the love of His people. He treasures that closeness.

God had wanted this from Israel in a previous era. Through Jeremiah, He says: "Thus says the Lord, 'I remember the devotion of your youth, your love as a bride, how you followed me in the wilderness, in a land now sown' " (Jeremiah 2:2). God reminisced over Israel's previous devotion, their simple love for Him. But now? "They did not say, 'Where is the Lord who brought us up from the land of Egypt?' " (Jeremiah 2:6). God grieved that they looked for Him no longer. Their first love was gone. They had, like the Ephesians, abandoned it. But God wanted it.

Christ searches for the life that maintains that devotion and love. Judas found fault with Mary's costly sacrifice in Simon's house. She had broken and poured out a valuable flask of fragrant oil upon Jesus, an act of extreme devotion and worship. Judas thought the oil could have been sold for nearly a year's worth of wages. He pretended to want to help the poor with these imagined proceeds. But Jesus rebuked the thought: "Truly, I say to you, wherever this gospel is proclaimed in the whole world, what she has done will also be told in memory of her" (Matthew 26:13). Christ loves that devotion. Christ loves our love.

As a father, I have always enjoyed it when my children made me a work of art. But I love it most when we all sit down, supplies in hand, and work together. They might still draw me a picture or paint me a painting, but this time we are together during the process. I am next to them; they are next to me. I much prefer this togetherness. The church in Ephesus had wandered from this. Their service for Christ was not with Him, not because of their love for Him. He preferred something different.

Solution

> Remember therefore from where you have fallen; re-
> pent, and do the works you did at first. (Revelation 2:5)

Jesus gave the Ephesian church a simple solution to that which ailed them, but the way of it might confound us. The way forward is not necessarily as easy as sparking up the first love again, going back to that. No, the question is, how does one go about getting that first love back? Jesus tells us. It is not by waiting for a lightning strike of love to hit us; instead, it is a simple process.

First, we must "Remember therefore from where you have fallen." Ephesus had to go back in their mind's eye to the time they had begun to fall from this simple devotion, and we must do the same. Perhaps it was a season of fruitfulness that got us off track. Perhaps it was a relationship that began to overtake our love for Christ. Perhaps it was a multitude of purchases that drowned out our devotion to Jesus. Perhaps clutter invaded our lives, and now there is no more room for Christ. Remember that moment when the departure began.

Second, we must "repent." Repent of what, we ask? Of how we currently are. Ephesus was to let contrition come upon them. They were not to brush these sins to the side but to turn from them. When we have identified where the lack of love crept in, we are to repent of it.

Third, we are to "do the works you did at the first." This is the final step. Notice, Jesus expects the first love to be found by doing the first works. This church had worked so hard for Jesus, but He tells them to go back to the "first work" works. Those works would lead them back into marital love.

At the beginning, when Ephesus got its start in Christ, the work was simple. They would pray to Christ. They would study the word of Christ. They would trust the power of Christ. They would submit to Christ. Their new life in Him was completely for Him, under Him, about Him. They lived lives of worship to Him. Now Jesus urges them to get back to that. Pray again. Study His Word again. Trust Him again. But in simple ways—not with complexity, but in simplicity.

This first work would turn into first love. Jesus said, "Where your treasure is, there your heart will be also" (Matthew 6:21). Our modern notion is that our works are an evidence of our hearts. They can be, but Jesus seems to indicate that our hearts will follow our treasure. How you spend your time and treasure will dictate where your heart goes. The Ephesian church was to get back to the simple basics of their faith in Christ. They could expect love to return as a result, like the blood flowing back into a limb that has fallen asleep. The feeling and life and fervency would return once the Ephesians decluttered themselves. A return to simple allegiance to Jesus would bring them life again.

The Christian life is not meant to be a highly complex endeavor. We mature, absolutely, but in all of life, we are to enjoy our Lord. Jesus invites Ephesus, and us, into that experience.

Warning

> If not, I will come to you and remove your lampstand
> from its place, unless you repent. (Revelation 2:5)

If Ephesus rejected this exhortation from Christ, He would "remove their lampstand" (Revelation 2:5). He is not threatening the removal of an entire church's salvation but merely explaining the results of a loveless devotion to the work. Without love for Christ, a church naturally loses its light and its potency. When first love is absent, we are bound to lose our light. The church is the light of the world, but without a love for Christ, that light dims.

This is not hard to imagine. Without that first love, a church might be very orthodox in doctrine but uncaring toward God and man. They will carry all the right beliefs but without a brokenheartedness over the condition of man.

Without that first love, they might defend the faith well but in a condescending way. An "us versus them" mentality will find a foothold, and the church will ostracize itself.

Without that first love, there might be a zeal for purity but without compassion for the lost. There will be much talk of a biblical sexual ethic but a lack of compassion for how a hurting humanity could find themselves outside that ethic. This loveless church sees how humankind has cast off God's restraint, but there is no mourning because of it.

This church is true and focused on its work, but it is without an attractiveness. The world must see a people in love with their Savior and Lord. The Ephesian church was orthodox in their beliefs . . . zealous for purity . . . strong defenders of the faith. Christ rejoiced over them for this. But their true effectiveness and light would flow from their love for Christ. They didn't need to subtract a thing, but love had to be added. Our true effectiveness depends on our devotion.

Promise

> He who has an ear, let him hear what the Spirit says to
> the churches. To the one who conquers I will grant to
> eat of the tree of life, which is in the paradise of God.
> (Revelation 2:7)

Each letter closes with a promise from Jesus to "the one who conquers" or "the overcomer." These promises are for believers. They are eternal in nature. Everything Jesus promises at this point in these letters is ours in Christ. Those who conquer are those who have saving faith in Christ. These promises are for Christians; they are the normal expectation of believers.

To the Ephesians, Christ says, "To the one who conquers I will grant to eat of the tree of life, which is in the paradise of God" (Revelation 2:7). This is helpful. Believers of all ages, just like the believers in Ephesus, need an eternal vision. Here, Jesus points forward by pointing backward. The tree of life had been in the garden of Eden but was held back from humankind after the fall. The tree of life reappears here and in the heavenly kingdom (Revelation 22). To eat of that tree will mean "healing for the nations," a most joyous experience.

Eternity is in our hearts, but Jesus attempts to put it more fully in our minds. The Ephesian church needed a vision for life in eternity with God. They had been fruitful for Him, but they needed to see His fruit for them. They would be in forever fellowship with Him without a massive work to engage in, resting in God. This time would come, and Christ points them toward it.

Although a forceful church worthy of deep commendation, the Ephesian church had left their earlier fervency for Christ. This letter stands as a plea for them to return. Oh, how Christ looked for renewed love from the Ephesians!

At the beginning of His letter to this church, Christ describes Himself as the One who held the stars of the churches in His right hand. He walks among the seven golden lampstands. Earlier in Revelation, Christ had shown John the meaning of these symbols. The stars were the angels (or messengers) of the churches, while the lampstands were the churches themselves. So when Jesus describes himself this way, He is pointing to His relationship with the church. He holds the leaders. He roams in the midst of the congregation.

In other words, Jesus sees Himself in close connection to the church in Ephesus. He wants to know them and for them to know Him. His description of Himself was His prescription for the Ephesians. It is as if He says, "I am nearby, Ephesians. I walk in your midst. I am closer than you think."

Christ calls for His bride. Perhaps you've found you've drifted from your first love. Perhaps your earlier fascination with Christ and His cross has waned. Repent! Return! Rekindle the fire by ruminating afresh on His glorious gospel of grace. He loves you, and you must think upon His great love if you've any hope of returning to the love you had for Him at the first.

CHAPTER 3

Smyrna

Mothers know the cries of their children. At a busy park, a mother can discern the distant cry of her child, separating the sound from all the other children's voices. Not only that, but they often can tell what the cry means. A hurt, a pain, a frustration—so often a mother knows.

Jesus knows the cry of His people. He hears the painful cries of His children. Throughout the world, when His people suffer, He sees and knows. He hurts for and with them. Christians suffer in various ways, but persecution is a significant category of Christian suffering. We all endure trials, but some endure arrests, beatings, or even death for the faith. This has always been the case, as our earliest days were rooted in various forms of religious persecution. The apostles suffered and died for the faith, and the early believers they ministered to were often persecuted as well.

The church is Smyrna was a hurting church. They had come under the pressure of persecution in their town. They suffered immensely for their faith. Jesus, in his letter to them, comforts them with the fact of his resurrection and the knowledge of what they are enduring. He also commends them for their real wealth, exhorting them not to fear and to be faithful. Finally, Christ promises them the ultimate crown and victory.

Description of Smyrna

Smyrna was a prominent city. Initiated by Alexander the Great some three hundred years before Christ, Smyrna was a beautiful and proud city. Rich because of trade, their hallmark was their devotion to the Roman emperors, having led the charge in the worship of the emperors.

Their worship of the Caesars began when they built the first temple to Dea Roma, the goddess (spirit) of Rome, in 196 BC. In AD 23, they won the right to build the first temple to worship Tiberius Caesar. By the time John wrote Revelation, Domitian had demanded worship, and Smyrna had obliged. They had gone from the worship of Rome to the worship of her dead emperors to the worship of her living emperors—all in a rather brief period of time. They had plunged headlong into Rome, devoted to her through and through.

This was all problematic to the church as the gospel spread there. One could not hold to both the lordship of Christ and the lordship of Caesar—at least not in the way Smyrna had come to practice Caesar's lordship. Theirs was a worship, and the Christian could not partake in it. No man should ever receive a Christian's worship, including the emperor.

As a testament to the hostility this conflict would cause in Smyrna, we have the historical record of the death of a pastor there, a man named Polycarp. He was apparently a disciple of John. When he was eighty-six years old, he was burned at the stake in Smyrna for his unwavering faith in Christ. The record of his martyrdom is of the fantastic variety. He received a preparatory vision of his suffering and bold confidence in the face of his tormentors. Burned alive, Polycarp was an incredible witness for Christ.

Perhaps Polycarp was emblematic of the church in Smyrna. Christ exhorts them in this letter, "Do not fear what you are about to suffer" (Revelation 2:10). They were about to go through some pain for Christ. The eventual death of one of their pastors seems to embody this pain.

Description of Jesus

> And to the angel of the church in Smyrna write: "The words of the first and the last, who died and came to life." (Revelation 2:8)

In the midst of this anticipated pain, Christ describes Himself to the church in Smyrna. His description is their prescription, for the church in all ages must feast on Christ. He reminds them He is "the first and the last, who died and came to life." The title "the first and the last" is borrowed from the Old Testament book of Isaiah (44:4, 44:6, 48:12). There it was used to describe God. Christ is God who became flesh. Jesus wanted the Smyrnan church to know that in His flesh, He died. But He did not remain dead, for He came back to life.

It is not hard to see how this was designed to impress and comfort the church in Smyrna. On the brink of suffering, wondering if they might die, they needed to see the power of Christ in overcoming death. It is as if Christ says to them, "I've been to the depths of pain and suffering, all the way to the most brutal of deaths, but I came back from even that. You too will overcome."

Smyrna needed this part of Christ's nature like parched earth needs water. The resurrection of Christ could impart sanity to the fearful minds in Smyrna, just as it can fortify a mind today. As Paul said to the Corinthians, "Christ has been raised from the dead, the firstfruits of those who have fallen asleep. For as by a man came death, by a man has come also the resurrection of the dead" (1 Corinthians 15:20–21). Christ's resurrection was first, and theirs would come later. This knowledge stood as a source of great encouragement to the suffering church in Smyrna.

Believers are helped through trials, including severe persecution, by digesting the truth of Christ's resurrection. When Lazarus died, Jesus told Lazarus's sister, Martha, "I am the resurrection and the life. Whoever believes in me, though he dies, yet shall he live, and everyone who lives and believes in me shall never die" (John 11:25–26). His statement feels initially like a contradiction. He says believers will die ("though he dies"), but then He says that believers "shall never die." According to Christ, we live and die . . . but never die. How can it be both? Only by the power of His resurrection. It has turned our deaths into mere sleep; the second death has no power over us. Jesus asked Martha, and we ask ourselves, "Do you believe this?" (John 11:26).

Comfort

> I know your tribulation and your poverty (but you are rich) and the slander of those who say that they are Jews and are not, but are a synagogue of Satan. (Revelation 2:9)

At this point in His letter, Jesus begins to encourage the church in Smyrna. For them, the knowledge of His resurrection was good medicine, but it was also an orientation to their future— and their immediate future was scary. Christ would speak to it.

Their "right now" situation needed His attention, and He provides it. Christ does this by telling them He knows. "I know your situation," Christ says. Jesus begins to comfort this church by announcing His intimate knowledge of all they are enduring. He sees three specific things in the church in Smyrna.

First, He knew their tribulation. Tribulation is a trial that is caused by pressure. Like grapes under the pressure of the winepress, so the believers in Smyrna were under immense pressure due to the persecution of that hour. Their tribulation wasn't mere Christian trial, nor was it the great tribulation, but it was the tribulation that hits the church during times of persecution. The other cities may have experienced hate and lower grades of persecution, but the Smyrna church had a heightened degree of the pressure of persecution to deal with.

Second, He knew their poverty. They had become financially poor—the word He uses speaks of deep poverty—likely because of the persecution. They couldn't get the good jobs, good schools, or good contracts. Their community financially persecuted them. Their lack of allegiance to the emperor had precipitated a witch hunt. This campaign against the believers in Smyrna had led to the church's poverty.

Third, He knew the slander they were enduring. It appears to have come from the Jewish community in Smyrna. In some cities the Jews were open to the gospel, or at least able to dwell congenially with the church, but not in Smyrna. Jesus calls them a synagogue of Satan, for they weren't living out the true Jewish ideals found in the Old Testament. They had actively engaged themselves in spreading lies about the Christian church in Smyrna. Jesus saw it. He knew of it.

All of this is unsurprising to the reader of the New Testament. Jesus had warned His disciples time and time again of a coming age of persecution—"I have said all these things to you to keep you from falling away. They will put you out of the synagogues. Indeed, the hour is coming when whoever kills you will think he is offering service to God" (John 16:1–2). Hatred for the church had hit Smyrna, and it continues to hit various Christian communities throughout the world.

But in all this, what did Jesus mean when He said He knew of their tribulation, poverty, and slander?

He knew, of course, because from His exalted and eternal position, He could see the events of their lives. There was not a hair on their heads unknown to Him (Matthew 10:30). His thoughts toward them were more than the sands of the sea (Psalm 139:17–18). He lives to make intercession for His people, and the church at Smyrna was no different (Hebrews 7:25). He was their Advocate (1 John 2:1). He could see everything happening to them. He knew.

But perhaps His knowledge runs deeper than a mere comprehension. Jesus seems to have known of their situation because He had lived it in the days of His earthly pilgrimage as well. No one has known persecution quite like Christ; they took Him to the cross! It was a bizarre hatred that flowed from the religious leaders of His day, rooted in jealousy. His human life began on the run because of the persecution of Herod, and His earthly life ended with the cross. The Smyrna church was merely tasting the persecution endured by Christ.

Jesus had also experienced the poverty of the Smyrna church. "Foxes have holes, and birds of the air have nests, but the Son of Man has nowhere to lay his head" (Luke 9:58). He had lived a life on the run; He had known what it was to be poor. Born in a stable, sleeping His first nights in a feeding trough, Jesus understood the poverty of the Smyrna church.

Jesus had also experienced the slander they were enduring. Things were said of Christ that were entirely untrue. "He has a demon," shouted one. "He is out of His mind," shouted another. They called Him a glutton and a drunkard. Blasphemy was the charge that got Him killed, but all He'd done was truthfully call God His Father. Jesus suffered long through slander. He knew what the Smyrnan church faced.

Perhaps it is comforting to you to remember that Christ has endured the trials and tribulations of this life. No matter what Smyrna faced, and no matter what you face, Jesus Christ has experienced it to a greater degree. His temptations, His trials, His burdens, His heartbreaks, His losses—all of it was of the deepest variety. He looks at us and knows—partly because He sees, but mostly because He endured worse.

Praise

But you are rich. (Revelation 2:9)

In the midst of this comfort, the Lord has a brief word of praise for the church in Smyrna. He has no word of rebuke for them, as He does with most of the other churches. They were a fellowship that needed no corrective word. Perhaps this silence speaks volumes. Remember, they'd been persecuted. Christ did not admonish them at all. Perhaps this means they hadn't responded inappropriately to the persecution. They had been as Christ: "He was oppressed, and he was afflicted, yet he opened not his mouth; like a lamb that is led to the slaughter, and like a sheep that before its shearers is silent, so he opened not his mouth" (Isaiah 53:7).

Christ had turned the other cheek, and so had this church. There-fore, no rebuke.

But Jesus does have one small word of praise for them. For other churches, His praise is often longer, more detailed. We've al-ready seen the multifaceted praise of the church in Ephesus. One can find eight or nine (or more) stand-alone words of praise for them. But not for Smyrna. The praise is spoken succinctly, with razor precision. It is simple: "But you are rich."

He said it to them immediately after acknowledging their pov-erty. He saw all their financial ruin but also saw something more. In the midst of material poverty, they were spiritually wealthy. They might not have had earthly riches, but they had the true riches. With a whisper, He announces the good He sees in them. They are the wealthy church, in actuality.

This statement from Christ will fall in direct contrast with His later statement to the church in Laodicea. That church thought they were wealthy. "For you say, I am rich, I have prospered, and I need nothing, not realizing that you are wretched, pitiable, poor, blind, and naked" (Revelation 3:17). These are words no church wants to hear from Christ. They thought they were rich but had nothing. But the church in Smyrna had nothing and was rich. They had the true riches, those that cannot decay, rust, fade, or become stolen (Matthew 6:19–20).

They might have been the poorest, but they were the wealthiest. One day, during Jesus's earthly life, a man came to Him, asking Christ to settle a familial dispute: "Teacher, tell my brother to di-vide the inheritance with me" (Luke 12:13). After telling the man that "one's life does not consist in the abundance of his posses-sions," Jesus told everyone a parable (Luke 12:15). In His story there was a wealthy man whose barn had grown full, meaning he had no room to store additional harvests. The man pondered the problem, deciding to tear down his barns and replace them with larger barns. His aim was simple: store up enough so that in his future years He could "eat, drink, [and] be merry" (Luke 12:19).

To the listener of the parable it may have sounded like a dream scenario, the life everyone looks for—comfort and ease in the final stage of life. But Jesus shocked those who heard the parable by concluding: "But God said to him, 'Fool! This night your soul is required of you, and the things you have prepared, whose will they be?' So is the one who lays up treasure for himself and is not rich toward God" (Luke 12:20–21).

This was the Smyrna church. They had no barns. They had no earthly security. But they were rich toward God. Had we known them we might've prayed for them to be delivered from persecution, to be provided for with abundance. But they might have prayed for us to know God the way they knew God. Through the trials and pain and persecution, they had learned to depend on God alone. They had nowhere else to turn. For this, they had a rich experience with the Living God. Theirs was a closeness and intimacy and power that is exceptional.

Jesus, of course, embraced poverty for us that we might have richness with God. "For you know the grace of our Lord Jesus Christ, that though he was rich, yet for your sake he became poor, so that you by his poverty might become rich" (2 Corinthians 8:9).

Jesus Christ makes way for a deeper and richer life than is commonly offered to us. Humankind runs around trying to find meaning in satisfactory things like work or wealth or family or friendships. We also try to find meaning in sinful things like sexual license and hateful causes and divisions. But Christ provides the possibility of life beyond all that. He makes way for deeper meaning. Paul the Apostle, a man touched deeply by Christ, described his life as "having nothing, yet possessing everything" (2 Corinthians 6:10). This was the church in Smyrna; they had nothing but had everything, for they were rich in Christ.

The suffering church might be poor, but they are wealthier than the comfortable church. They have power from Christ and intimacy with Christ. Perhaps understanding this would help us to get out of our comfort zones—to get uncomfortable. We need not choose persecution but rather choose obedience. As we obey, we might find ourselves thrust into discomfort. But Christ is there in the discomfort, distributing the true riches.

Would you be truly wealthy? Do you desire the true riches? Know that the enemy of our souls has a few constant strategies, and one of them is the delusion of riches. Money has been the easy path toward tepidness in the Christian life, but Smyrna had true wealth. We cannot (usually) choose persecution, but we do choose paths which might take us there. But we must remember what true wealth looks like. There are greater treasures in store for those who experience discomfort for the cause of Christ.

Jesus said, "Take up your cross, die, and follow me." This sounds painful until you live it a little. Then you discover it is the easy yoke and the light burden. To seek to save your life is, in actuality, a most painful life. But to, with Smyrna, be discomforted for your allegiance to Christ provides us with the greater riches.

Exhortation

> Do not fear what you are about to suffer. Behold, the devil is about to throw some of you into prison, that you may be tested, and for ten days you will have

tribulation. Be faithful unto death, and I will give you
the crown of life. (Revelation 2:10)

After identifying with His suffering church, Christ exhorts His
suffering church. The word He gives them is ominous, as He alludes to a future season of suffering. He has no word of escape
for them. Instead, He tells them not to fear the coming time of
suffering—a time that would include a period of imprisonment,
testing, and tribulation.

Many have wondered at the description of this coming time of
prison, testing, and tribulation. Christ said it would last for ten
days. Interpreters have run wild with this phrase. Would it be ten
waves of Roman persecution? Was He symbolically speaking of
ten years or, strangely enough, 240 years? Was He simply men-
tioning a short or set period of time? To what did Christ refer?

I will not be surprised if, in glory, the Smyrna church replies to
the interpreters of every age that some of them were thrown into
a Smyrna jail for ten days. It might be that black and white.

Whatever the meaning, the warning from Christ loomed over
them. They might have wanted Him to say, "Don't fear it, for I
will see you out of it." But this is not Christ's word. Instead, He
says, "Don't fear it, for I will see you *through* it." He would not
give them a way of escape but a way of endurance.

How can Christ say such a thing? How could they be fearless in
the face of this coming danger? Let us consider two incorrect
answers, followed by a correct one.

First, they were not fearless due to a lack of suffering. I've already mentioned this. They knew the road in front of them was
hard. They likely already sensed this, but now Christ confirms it.

Without a promise of escape, they were now prepared for battle. They put on their helmets and moved forward. So the lack of fear Christ encouraged wasn't based on a lack of pain. No, pain was in their future.

Second, they were not fearless due to their current attitude. The modern or Western church might sometimes think of the persecuted church as superhuman. We like to hear tales of their bold exploits in the face of danger. Ever since the disciples were released from that first imprisonment two thousand years ago, Christians have loved hearing of the boldness of the church in the face of persecution. But Christ exhorts the Smyrnan church this way precisely because they weren't bold. Their natural state was that of fear.

I recall a conversation with a friend who ministers to believers in nations where Christianity is outlawed. He described for me the fear that often comes upon them. They struggle as they fight for survival. The boldness of the Spirit often helps them, but they are in need of exhortations like this from Christ. No, Christ didn't command fearlessness from Smyrna because they didn't have fear . . . but because they were steeped in it. What they were about to face was frightful.

So what is the correct answer? How could Christ tell them to have fearlessness in the face of peril? Because He had endured peril and come out of it resurrected, glorified. He had passed through the pain, embraced it fully, and succeeded. He knew the human element of fear, having felt it fully in the Garden of Gethsemane. "Father, if it be possible, let this cup pass from me," was His cry (Matthew 26:39). But as intense as the cross had been, He had survived. He lived. He rose. He endured.

In the same way, Christ could exhort them toward fearlessness because He was living proof they would get through to glory. Christ has endured the pain. He was not unscathed but scathed, yet a resurrected state was His.

Again, we remember Christ's description of Himself to the church in Smyrna. He "died and came to life." This description should fill them—and us—with great hope in the face of suffering, especially persecution.

Remember the attitude of the early church. After their first real appointment with persecution, they rejoiced for being found worthy to suffer for the name of Christ (Acts 5:41). They had fellowshipped with Jesus in His suffering, and it was sweet. This caused them to rejoice.

We would do well to remember the effect persecution had on our original church family. In the book of Acts, persecution was seen as a terror to the church, but it ultimately served the purposes of God, in the same manner that Judas's betrayal had. God had told them to go to the whole world; persecution helped force the going.

Christ also told them to "be faithful unto death, and I will give you the crown of life." Through the persecution, they were to keep their strong conviction. The early church, on tasting persecution, prayed for boldness, not deliverance, and Christ seems to reiterate this focus. "Get faithfulness," He tells them.

Noah was a man cut from Smyrnan cloth. Christ asked much of him in the building of that ark. Over and over again it says Noah "did all that God had commanded him" (Genesis 6:22, 7:5, 16). This Noahic faithfulness ought to be our strong desire.

Only Christ could ask us to be faithful unto death, the ultimate sacrifice. He made the ultimate sacrifice, and He asks this of His church if need be. No man could ever ask—or rightfully get—that brand of allegiance. But Christ—with His infinite love and grace, with His eternal promises—can. To live faithfully to Him, obediently at all costs, makes the utmost sense when Christ is considered fully.

The crown of life was in store for those in Smyrna who endured faithfully to the end. This is the crown of the winning athlete, a trophy of accomplishment. There must be a sweet savor to the fulfillment of this desire. They had run their race, and now the trophy was theirs. This is the promise Christ makes to this persecuted church.

This promise was important for the persecuted church to hear, for their Christianity felt like a race, a competition taking every ounce of effort and concentration to complete. They were likely tiring and in need of a reminder of a glorious finish. Should they endure, a crown awaited them.

Often, we are made able to endure simply through focusing on the reward of Christ. To hear His affirming voice over our lives, to receive His crown and reward, serves as a motivation to endure in the here and now.

This church might not have been the most notable in their day, but Christ saw them as winners.

Promise

> He who has an ear, let him hear what the Spirit says to
> the churches. The one who conquers will not be hurt
> by the second death. (Revelation 2:11)

Finally, we come to our word for the overcomers, the conquerors. Again, these words are for all true believers. Every letter concludes with a promise for the conqueror, and every promise is eternal in nature. Believers get these promises by faith in Christ.

The promise here, appropriately, is a victory over the second death. The second death is hell, the lake of fire (Revelation 20:14, 21:8). The devil who persecuted them for ten days would be hurt by that second death, but not the church in Smyrna.

This promise stood in obvious contrast to the first death. They, like us, all had to pass through the first death. Many of them did so in a brutal way due to the persecution. Even though that death might hurt them, the second death could not.

Believers in every generation are thankful for the presence of this letter to the church in Smyrna. If persecuted, the letter has given hope. If unpersecuted, the letter has given perspective. In all cases, the letter has given deeper love for the most hurting of churches, because the same hate that nailed Christ to His cross exists today. Let us, as the church in Smyrna, be rich in the best categories, rich toward God.

CHAPTER 4

Pergamum

The Bible uses many metaphors and similes to describe itself. It speaks of itself like a fire burning within (Jeremiah 20:9). Its flames are unquenchable, so we must proclaim it. It speaks of itself as a hammer (Jeremiah 23:29). It chisels and breaks, shaping those who put themselves under its influence. It speaks of itself as a river bringing life to those planted by it (Psalm 1). It flows, nourishing all who plant themselves near its banks. It speaks of itself as cleansing water (Ephesians 5:26). It washes us clean from the grime of life.

One image used of the Bible is that of a mirror. James writes, "If anyone is a hearer of the word and not a doer, he is like a man who looks intently at his natural face in a mirror. For he looks at himself and goes away and at once forgets what he was like" (James 1:23–24). A mirror reflects. We use mirrors to see what is reflected so that we might look our best. We discover blemishes and flaws in the mirror. We then attend to them. God's Word is a mirror for His people, and without it, we drift off course. Our hearts might deceive us, but the Word of God is an accurate and genuine mirror, exposing our souls.

The church in Pergamum needed this type of relationship with the Word of Christ. They were, for the most part, a great church. Jesus commends them heartily. Still, a fatal blemish existed in the church there. There was a segment that held to various forms of teaching that could kill the church. Jesus will hold up the mirror of His word to the Pergamum church, showing them the error. If they chose to, they could then correct the error within.

The error of Pergamum was accepting teaching they should have rejected. It wasn't, as we will see, accepted by the entire church—nor even a majority. Still, it was this harmful and inaccurate teaching that was gaining ground in the church there. It wasn't a secondary issue, something the church could agree to disagree on, but something more vital than that. This line of teaching, if accepted, would crush the power of the church in Pergamum. Their strength would be reduced to nothingness if this teaching gained ground. It was lethal.

A good Scripture to think of regarding the church in Pergamum is found in the last chapter of all of Paul's great works. In his final days, passing the baton to Timothy, Paul told him to preach the Word. Stick to that. But why? "For the time is coming when people will not endure sound teaching, but having itching ears they will accumulate for themselves teachers to suit their own passions, and will turn away from listening to the truth and wander off into myths" (2 Timothy 4:3–4).

Some in Pergamum had done the very thing Paul warned Timothy about. They could not abide by sound teaching, for that takes endurance. They grew weary in that race. In need of a jolt of artificial energy, they turned, as many do, to "teachers to suit their own passions." They had accumulated these teachers. They had turned away from listening to the truth. Again, this wasn't what everyone in the Pergamum church had done, but some. These teachings had floated their way, and they merged perfectly with their own passions, so they were deceived. To this, Jesus will speak.

Description of Pergamum

Pergamum (or Pergamos) sounds as if it were a fascinating place. Each of these seven cities had various forms of religiosity. But Pergamum was most experimental and experiential in its religiosity. The city had temples to three Roman emperors, so the Smyrna error was in their town also, as they worshiped Rome and her Caesars. Additionally, she harbored temples to four gods: Zeus, Dionysus, Athena, and Asclepius were all honored there.

It is Asclepius's temple that sounds most bizarre. It was set up as a spa-like center, and snake worship abounded there. The desire in his temple was not fertility, as with Diana, but healing. The snake on the pole had become their god. They sought healings of various sorts there. Humans are prone to seek physical healing at any cost, and the culture in Pergamum was no different. When they slept in the temple, they hoped they would receive nighttime dreams of healing. Some even hoped one of the snakes who slithered freely throughout the temple would brush up against them, all with hopes of a supernatural healing. One cannot help but think of the healing power of Christ found in the gospels, which was extended to the church in Acts. Those miracles were mostly signs, of course, pointing to the future age when all believers in Christ will find permanent healing. The Pergamum culture was ripe for the Ultimate Healer, Jesus Christ.

Beyond the religious realm, Pergamum must have had a deep intellectual component as well. Eventually they would build a large two-hundred-thousand-volume library, immense for that era.

During John's day, Pergamum already displayed the beginnings of a voracious information appetite.

When you put all their books and all their religious ideas together, what you have in Pergamum is a community that is open to anything. They would try new ideas and teachings, unafraid of even the most bizarre. Deception there was high. And this attitude seems to have snaked its way into the church there also. They were open, ready for new ideas to suit their passions, as we will see.

Description of Jesus

> And to the angel of the church in Pergamum write: "The words of him who has the sharp two-edged sword."(Revelation 2:12)

When Jesus described Himself to this church, He chose the sword. Remember, John had seen the glorified Christ at the opening of Revelation. The double-edged sword had protruded from Christ's mouth. Later in Revelation, this sword would be used for judgment. Here, for Pergamum, the sword could be used for surgery, but if elective surgery were refused, it would be used for judgment.

One fascinating element of this sharp sword for Pergamum is related to the city's history. Rome held the sword, ultimately, and capital punishment belonged to Rome. Occasionally, Rome would give a city the sword, meaning the city could enact the death penalty with Rome's oversight. This was Rome's way of loaning their authority to a worthy town. This sword had been given to Pergamum. They had an authoritative sword and word there.

So Christ's sword is telling for the church. It is almost as if Christ is saying, "Your governmental authorities have the sword, but I have the true sword. Their word is authoritative, but mine is more so." What Pergamum legalized might not be legal for the believers, for they were under a stronger authority.

This concept is helpful to believers in various cultures. We must know that the Word of Christ is our final authority. Our government might even allow, within its laws, various behaviors that are questionable. But the believer goes back to Christ and asks, "Is this for me, my Lord?"

The government might tell people who they are allowed to marry, but what does Christ say? The government might tell people what they are allowed to ingest, but what does Christ say? The government might tell people what they are allowed to preach, but what does Christ say? He, for the believer, is the final Word and authority.

Praise

> I know where you dwell, where Satan's throne is. Yet you hold fast my name, and you did not deny my faith even in the days of Antipas my faithful witness, who was killed among you, where Satan dwells. (Revelation 2:13)

Jesus saw they lived where Satan's throne was. But what are we to make of this statement? It might seem bizarre to the modern mind to think of demons and devils and angels, but this is part of the grand deception. Our fictional art is saturated with the demonic, supernatural, and spiritual. Could it be that the knowledge we've suppressed—the knowledge that there is more than we can see—is showing up in our art, our fiction?

The question, of course, is what does Jesus mean when he announces Pergamum as the place where Satan's throne is—the place where Satan dwells? Some have thought this to be a reference to the altar of Zeus in the city. Others have thought it alludes to the old emperor worship found there. Still others have believed it a reference to the Roman governors who used to frequent Pergamum. Some have thought Jesus is pointing to the worship of Asclepius's snake image, which would be similar to the serpent in Eden, who was Satan.

But I see no reason not to see this as a plain statement from Christ. He writes these letters to the angels of the seven churches, so every letter is already steeped in the supernatural and unseen realm. Why would it be bizarre for Christ to point out that the headquarters of Satan—at that time—were in Pergamum? We know Satan is not omnipresent; that is an attribute only God possesses. If Satan is here, he cannot be there. Only God is everywhere. But Satan does oversee a network of principalities and powers: "For we do not wrestle against flesh and blood, but against the rulers, against the authorities, against the cosmic powers over this present darkness, against the spiritual forces of evil in the heavenly places" (Ephesians 6:12). Perhaps, at the time of John, Satan oversaw his operation from Pergamum. He had been cast from heaven, but he does not live in hell. The earth is his in-between, and Pergamum may have been his residence at that time.

If this is the case, it is fascinating to consider. Pergamum was not a place of widespread squalor. No, it was a refined culture. Abundance, wealth, intellect, and a general spiritual openness were there. Pergamum could have been where Satan headquartered, where he administered his evil plots and forces.

However we take Christ's statements about Satan's throne, it would have been a deep comfort to the Pergamum church to realize that Jesus knew the spiritual darkness of the place they lived in. Pergamum was no comfortable place to live the Christian life. There was pressure and opposition, which came from more than their flesh or the natural man; it was spiritual and dark. In that place, Jesus commended them. They had held fast to His name and had not denied their faith in Him. There was even a moment when one of them, an otherwise unknown biblical character named Antipas, was killed for his Christianity. Even when the hostility in Pergamum grew to that intensity, they had not turned from the Lord. They endured.

They might not have endured the same level of persecution the church in Smyrna had (or would), but it was persecution nonetheless. Modern believers might read of persecution in Acts and feel the opposition we experience today insignificant in comparison. We might read about the persecuted church in recent ages. Many believers have lost their lives for their faith in the last hundred years or so, and today, many suffer for being in Christ. We read or hear of them and feel our lower levels of persecution are trite . . . nothing.

Pergamum, though no Smyrna, felt the pressure and pain. Whatever is hard for you is hard for you. You might gain perspective when seeing someone else's deeper struggle, but it cannot completely delete the struggle you are in. Parents with many children might look back on the days when they had only one child and smile at the ease of those days. But when they went through those days, they were hard, for they had never had even one child up to that point.

In this pressure, Pergamum stood. If you dwell in a dark place, a place hostile to the gospel, know that Christ knows. He sees the hostility and the deeper reasons for it. He knows the spiritual forces that are against you, against the church, against the truth. He watches, and as you endure, He is pleased.

Correction

> But I have a few things against you: you have some there who hold the teaching of Balaam, who taught Balak to put a stumbling block before the sons of Israel, so that they might eat food sacrificed to idols and practice sexual immorality. So also you have some who hold the teaching of the Nicolaitans. (Revelation 2:14–15)

Though the church in Pergamum was strong, they had a dangerous error. This is where the mirror of Christ's Word is going to expose a cancer in their midst. Not everyone held to these teachings, as Christ was careful to say "you have some there who hold the teaching of. . ." But the general church body needed to know what was lurking in the corner of their fellowship. Some in Pergamum had received demonic teachings.

The two teachings Christ mentions are the teaching of Balaam and the Nicolaitans. I will take the second first, for we know little of the Nicolaitan error. Perhaps it developed later into Gnosticism, but what it was at this stage is unclear. But Jesus said, "So also you have some who hold" this pernicious doctrine. Perhaps this indicates a strong connection between the doctrine of the Nicolaitans with the doctrine of Balaam. Perhaps they are similar—almost one and the same.

We know much, however, of the doctrine of Balaam. Other New Testament passages decry its error, calling it the "way" and "error" of Balaam (2 Peter 2:15, Jude 11). But what was this teaching?

Balaam himself was not alive at the time John wrote; he was from the Old Testament era. After the Exodus, when God's people were wandering on their way to Canaan, they came to Moabite territory. Balak, the king of Moab, hated Israel. He tried to hire a sorcerer prophet named Balaam to pronounce a curse upon Israel because Israel was too mighty for him (Numbers 22:1–6). God Himself announced to Balaam the impossibility of that invitation. He was not to curse Israel, "for they are blessed" (Numbers 22:12). So, begrudgingly, Balaam refused the offer. He would not curse Israel. Unfortunately, the story did not end there.

Balaam continued to think about that money, the offer from Balak. He wanted it. His covetous heart got the best of him, so he went to Balak even though God had forbidden it. God opposed Balaam on his journey, but he still went. Once he arrived, three times he attempted to pronounce a curse on Israel. It is strange to us, but he tried to put some kind of spell on Israel. He wanted them to suffer some sort of supernatural disaster.

The strangest thing happened, however. Every time he tried to curse Israel, a blessing would flow out his mouth toward them. Instead of cursing, he blessed. This wasn't what king Balak had paid for. Balaam failed in his pursuit, his mission, and this is where the story ends.

The next scene, found in Numbers, is where the teaching of Balaam comes in. After blessing the people three times, Balaam leaves the scene, but what we read next is terrible. Some in Israel began worshipping the Moabite god, Baal, and engaging sexually with the Moabite women, which was forbidden. God then breaks out against them, killing many in His judgment. These were, after all, His covenant people. Their behavior was in violation of their covenant with God and had endangered their part in His Messianic promises.

But what does this have to do with Balaam and his teaching? We learn later in Numbers. One day, Moses saw Moabite women enter the camp again. This was abhorrent to him. He said, "Behold, these, on Balaam's advice, caused the people of Israel to act treacherously against the Lord in the incident of Peor, and so the plague came among the congregation of the Lord" (Numbers 31:16). This comment from Moses fills in some details about the previous event. Why had the Moabite women gone into Israel's camp? Because Balaam had counseled king Balak to send them. Balaam's curse didn't work to curse Israel, but his counsel did, for Israel's sin caused God to lift His blessing off of them in judgment.

This has been the age-old strategy of Satan toward God's people in every era. He knows he cannot harm God's people. He knows they are blessed. So he focuses his attention on corrupting their morals, joining them with the passions of the world and their flesh. When this occurs, God will deal with them. Though Satan cannot touch them, God can. His holiness demands it.

This is where the cross is massive, looming gloriously over our lives. Jesus took the curse for us. Satan thought the sin of humanity an irreparable breach. God's holiness demanded eternal separation from man—but not from Christ. He took the curse, the sin, the wrath, the judgment, so that we might be restored to God.

So some in the Pergamum church had adopted a Balaam-like teaching. As I said, Balaam is dead and gone, but his teaching remains even today. The teaching is simple: corrupt yourself, fulfill your desires.

But how does this teaching get an audience in the first place? This is where Christ's word to the Pergamum church is powerful. In explaining it to them, Jesus says Israel (and some in Pergamum) had received Balaam's teaching "so that they might eat food sacrificed to idols and practice sexual immorality."

Do not miss this, for it is an error in our modern time. Some in Pergamum had received a doctrine because of their desires. They saw the festivals and ceremonies and illicit sex, and they wanted it. After desiring it, they found a doctrine to justify it.

Is this not a constant temptation for God's people? We have desires. We want to feel accepted by our society. When that desire grows, it can be tempting to adopt doctrines that enable that acceptance. The temptation is constant. Humankind loves to craft a system of worship and belief that suits their desires. This has always been. Start with a desire; craft a doctrine. This is an honest word from Christ. They hadn't started with a doctrine in Peor or in Pergamum; they had started with a desire. This is often the case today as well.

And, of course, this doctrine enslaved Israel and some in Pergamum and will enslave many today. We are helped by understanding just how different we are as God's people. The Bible calls us pilgrims and sojourners and citizens of heaven. This is not our home. We are to come out from among the world and be separate. We do not operate "in the passion of lust like the Gentiles who do not know God" (1 Thessalonians 4:5). We've spent enough of our past lifetime living that way. We are now new. No desire is worth changing a doctrine for. That is cancer.

As believers, we must be on guard against the unredeemed portions of our hearts. Our desires might tempt us to pursue doctrines that fit our longings, but this is not the way of Christ. He graciously and lovingly looks upon the condition of man and speaks truth to us. He will tell us what our hearts often do not want to hear. He will brazenly and clearly—without any mixed motive—tell us what we need to hear. His Word is pure, while our hearts are not. Allow Christ to change your desires before you change His doctrine.

But there is another lesson to see in the Pergamum error. It is connected, as with the first, to the original Old Testament story of Balaam. He tried to curse the people. He attempted to prophesy doom upon them, but they were protected by the covenant God had made with Abraham, Isaac, and Jacob. They were His people—untouchable.

Still, though Balaam couldn't curse them, they managed to curse themselves. By joining sexually with the Moabites and engaging in their worship of Baal, Israel opened the door to God's discipline upon their lives. His wrath began to pour out, and many of them died. This only shows us that the stakes—in God's mind—were very high at that moment. They were a nation in danger of extinction because of their sexual sin with the Moabites. Rather than live as pilgrims, they were joining in, and when God's people join the world, they get swallowed up by it. But the Messiah, the Christ, the Savior of the world, had not yet come. But He must come, and only from Israel. In short, Israel's sin at that moment endangered the cross of Christ. The sin was so grave that the discipline would be severe.

But this outline of events helps us see another lesson in the Pergamum church. They might have believed the covenant God made with them meant they were untouchable, unable to be hurt. Like many today, they might have believed God would overlook their persistent sins because of His great covenant with them. They might have thought the cross made a way, gave license, to sin. Balaam's error exists today (Jude 11). The idea we can abuse grace has been around for as long as the cross of Christ. But we must resist. The beautiful position we've received in Christ compels us to move forward into experiential holiness—not backward into license. We have been set free.

Solution

> Therefore repent. If not, I will come to you soon and war against them with the sword of my mouth. (Revelation 2:16)

What the Pergamum church needed more than anything was a revival in the Scriptures, the Word of God. The sword protruding from the mouth of Christ was exactly what they needed. Either they would invite the Word in or He would judge them with it, but either way, the Word was needed.

Do we not need a revival in the Word of God? Does not our dependency on Internet search engines reveal that we know little of how to think biblically on a myriad of subjects in life?

In the Old Testament, a common enemy of Israel, especially during the era of the judges and early kings, was the Philistines. During Saul's reign, the Philistines removed every sword and even sharp metal instruments from the Israelites. When Israel needed a sharpened tool for farming or labor, they had to go to Philistine territory and pay a fee for sharpening. This was strategic. When the day of battle came, only Saul and his son Jonathan could produce swords. Everyone else was swordless.

Pray this will not be a picture of our modern churches—swordless, wordless, helpless, and defenseless. We must revive ourselves to His word, embracing it as the Word of Life. Let us teach it, discuss it, and apply it. Let it not collect the dust of neglect or the stain of misuse.

Pergamum needed to repent over having received such teaching and teachers. They needed to reject everything contrary to God's Word.

Promise

> He who has an ear, let him hear what the Spirit says to the churches. To the one who conquers I will give some of the hidden manna, and I will give him a white stone, with a new name written on the stone that no one knows except the one who receives it. (Revelation 2:17)

As He does with all the churches, Christ gives Pergamum an eternal promise. What would the true believers there receive? What blessings awaited the real disciples in Pergamum?

They'd receive hidden manna and a white stone with a new name written on that stone. Admittedly, these promises are more mysterious than any we've covered so far. Ephesus's tree of life and Smyrna's escape from the second death are clearer to us. But all of these promises to Pergamum seem to touch on identity and friendship, important for a church tempted in the way they were.

The original manna was the food miraculously given by God to Israel throughout their wilderness wanderings. It ceased once Israel entered into the Promised Land. There, they would go war and work for their food. In the wilderness, however, God would feed them directly. Every day—except the Sabbath—they went out and gathered the manna for that day. It spoke of continual, daily dependence upon God. But it was very personal. You collected the manna for yourself, not your nation.

The white stone has received various interpretations. Some have found historical references to the white stone as a special invitation, a symbol of acquittal after trial, a sign of victory after a battle, or a statement of freedom from slavery. Some have even seen it as a *tessera hospitalis*. This was a white stone two friends would split in two, and each would carry one half of the stone as a reminder of the close friendship. Each of these interpretations indicates intimacy and closeness.

The new name written on the stone came from Christ. All throughout Scripture He renamed those He loved. The future for the Pergamum believers was no different. He would name them with a name no one else knew. Again, this is intimate, close, personal.

With all this said, it seems these promises would help the Pergamum church regain a hope for Christ's identity and friendship. When one changes doctrines as Pergamum did, there is a resulting wavering of identity. But when Christ has named you and loved you, you become secure enough to keep doctrines that offend the modern man.

CHAPTER 5

Thyatira

I magine a father walking along a road with his child. They move silently. Then, almost abruptly, the father stops and grabs hold of his child's hand. He stoops and embraces the child. Then the father tells his child he loves them.

At that moment, the child *experiences* the love of the father as the father *expresses* his love. But the child is no more loved at that moment than at other times. That father has a stated position of love toward his child, but at that moment the child has felt it. The love has become personal.

Human beings are thirsty for love. Our hearts search for acceptance—we crave it. Believers, like that child, walk down the road of life firmly fixed in the love of God in Christ Jesus. Our position in the Father's love is secure. We need, however, to experience His love personally. To have our eyes opened to this love provides us with protection against error and vain living.

Notice the way Paul prayed for the Ephesian church: "That Christ may dwell in your hearts through faith—that you, being rooted and grounded in love, may have strength to comprehend with all the saints what is the breadth and length and height and depth, and to know the love of Christ that surpasses knowledge, that you may be filled with all the fullness of God" (Ephesians 3:17–19).

Our eyes must be opened to the love of Christ. You might know of Christ's love for you; it is His stated position. You look to the cross and you see the evidence of His love. But if your eyes aren't opened to this love, you might become vulnerable to error. You might try to quench your thirst for love by searching in the wrong places. You might open up to the error of some who were in the church in Thyatira. His love must be enough for you. If not, error awaits.

Some in the church in Thyatira had entered into that error. They had added a strain of false teaching to their belief in Christ. The most outward evidence of this false teaching was some version of "sexual immorality" and the eating of "meat sacrificed to idols." They had grown discontent with Christ. Jesus's love had not enraptured them, so they turned to another love. They added something because they weren't satisfied in Him.

In the later portions of this letter, Christ Himself will allude to this false teaching as "the deep things of Satan." They had likely gone around saying they had discovered the "deep things," and Christ wants to make sure to add His commentary that these "things" are of Satan. But through these statements, you can see where this church had gone. They thought they'd found some-thing better . . . something deeper . . . something more wonderful than Christ.

Description of Thyatira

Thyatira was a frontier city whose history was filled with forced subjection and capture. They had, for a time, been subject to Pergamum. Located about thirty-five miles inland, between

Pergamum and Sardis, Thyatira was likely the least significant of these seven cities. We have no biblical record of the beginnings of the church there. We can only assume the great evangelistic effort of the Ephesian church had led to gospel preaching in Thyatira. Some had believed, and a church was born.

The city itself was known for a multitude of trade guilds, making it a blue-collar kind of town. They produced much of what the other cities consumed. These guilds operated like modern workers' unions. Clothiers, bakers, tanners, potters, slave traders, dyers, shoemakers, coppersmiths—they were all represented in Thyatira. (Lydia, Paul's first convert in Europe, is noted as "a seller of purple goods" [Acts 16:14]; she was from Thyatira.) But these guilds each had a patron deity, which would present an obstacle for believers. To advance in their trade, they were confronted with false worship. Believers were subject to economic suffering as a result.

Description of Jesus

> And to the angel of the church in Thyatira write: "The words of the Son of God, who has eyes like a flame of fire, and whose feet are like burnished bronze." (Revelation 2:18)

Jesus described himself to this church as the "Son of God," a title He does not usually use for Himself, preferring instead to refer to Himself as the "Son of Man." The "Son of Man" title highlights the incarnation, but the "Son of God" title emphasizes His glory and divinity, and His divinity is what they needed. The church needed to recapture a vision of the glorious Son of God—to realize there is nothing and no one more deep and mysterious than Him. Why turn to the deep things of Satan when you have the deep things of God found in the Son of God? Why turn to the voice of Jezebel, the self-proclaimed prophetess, when you have the voice of the Son of God?

Jesus also described Himself as the One with eyes of fire and feet of burnished bronze. The eyes of fire, as we analyzed in the first chapter, indicate His perfect and complete vision. He sees—and knows—all things. The feet of burnished bronze speak to His perfect and pure judgments. This is a way for Christ to tell the Thyatiran church that He sees them completely, and His judgments about what He sees are right and true. His assessment is accurate.

This lesson was crucial for the Thyatiran church, just as it is for us. Jesus Christ is the ultimate judge who sees all with accuracy. Even if I had total vision, the ability to see all things, my interpretations of what I see would be rife with inaccuracies. Only God sees all and judges all with perfection.

The apostle Paul spoke of this to the Corinthian church. They had begun to take a judgmental position toward him, falling under the influence of false teachers. Paul explained to them that it was no major consideration for him to be judged by them or by any human court. Any of us might say something like this, but Paul meant it. And he went further, explaining that he did not even judge himself (1 Corinthians 4:3). This lack of self-judgment is not to be mistaken as a laziness regarding personal introspection; rather, it should be understood that Paul was not aware of anything against himself (1 Corinthians 4:4). In other words, he frequently examined his inner man, striving to have a clean conscience. But even though he couldn't find anything, he said, "I am not thereby acquitted. It is the Lord who judges me" (1 Corinthians 4:4). Paul saw Christ as the perfect judge, the One who saw Him completely and accurately. The Corinthians didn't judge well, and Paul couldn't judge himself well. Only Christ could authoritatively judge this man.

The church in Thyatira needed, at this moment, to hear the voice of their most perfect judge. He saw them, and he had a word of correction for them.

Praise

> I know your works, your love and faith and service and patient endurance, and that your latter works exceed the first. (Revelation 2:19)

Even though some in their midst had fatal flaws, Jesus notices the best in this church, which is a skill we would do well to acquire. He saw something good even where darkness existed.

"I know your works," He says, followed by a list of five beautiful marks of the Thyatira church. All of these marks are found in the nature and character of Christ; His Spirit had produced these elements in the Thyatira church.

First, He sees their love. Their agape (selfless and sacrificial) love is noted by the Lord. It is one thing to be gifted but quite another to love. Power and authority are fine, but love is preeminent. If we have not love, we are nothing, and we gain nothing (1 Corinthians 13:2–3). This church operated in a love strong enough for the compliment of Christ.

Second, He sees their faith. They had believed and trusted Christ—for salvation, to be certain, but also for life. They had trusted Christ in their day-to-day experiences, leaning on Him as they walked through life.

Third, He sees their service. They were, like the Ephesians, a working church. They took ministry to others seriously, and Christ notices this. They were willing to do the menial tasks, the dirty work. They attended to others. Christ came not to be served but to serve, and they had caught His spirit.

Fourth, He sees their patient endurance. He saw them stay calm under pressure, tranquil in the face of trial. The waves of life may have tossed about them, but they remained firm in their midst. Jesus is fond of this resolute endurance, for He praises it often, seemingly whenever He sees it. He endured patiently as He went to the cross; they had become like Him in their suffering. Jesus loved their patience.

Finally, He sees that their latter works exceed the first works. They had increased and grown in their work for the Lord. They were growing, moving forward. They weren't content with where they had come from but wanted to progress. None of the spiritual armor in Ephesians covers our backside, and the Thyatirans seemed to understand this. There is only one direction for the Christian—forward.

This is an impressive list of excellent attributes in a church Christ loved. They made the mistake of tolerating a false teacher, but these wonderful attributes must not be overlooked. Christ doesn't. He praises them. This praise would have encouraged them initially, but it has also stood as a statement to every generation of the church. His praise shows us what He values, what He adores. These attributes are precious in His sight. We would benefit to pray through them, asking our perfect judge how we are doing in love, faith, service, endurance, and progress.

Correction

> But I have this against you, that you tolerate that wom-
> an Jezebel, who calls herself a prophetess and is teach-
> ing and seducing my servants to practice sexual immo-
> rality and to eat food sacrificed to idols. (Revelation
> 2:20)

Here, Jesus utilizes His perfect vision of the church in Thyatira and confronts them for tolerating a specific line of teaching. They had tolerated Jezebel, a woman in the church who had declared some special revelation from God, naming herself as a proph-etess. She seduced some in the church to engage in sexual im-morality and the eating of food sacrificed to idols. This was His solitary, yet significant, complaint against the church of Thyatira.

Immediately, the reader wants to know the identity of Jezebel. Was she a Jewish oracle? Was she Lydia? Was she the pastor's wife? All of these ideas have been held to by some. Whoever she was, Jesus saw her as Jezebel. Similar to the teaching of Balaam to the church in Pergamum, this teaching of Jezebel was also rooted in the Old Testament. There, Jezebel is portrayed as one of the most wicked women in Israel's history.

After Saul, David began to sit on the throne in Israel. God prom-ised him an everlasting throne, but after his son Solomon and grandson Rehoboam, there was a civil divorce in Israel. Only two of the twelve tribes remained under David's descendants, while ten tribes formed a separate nation in the North. The South be-came known as Judah, while the North was ordinarily entitled Israel. There, in the North, to keep the people from returning to Judah's Jerusalem for worship, golden calves were introduced. Thus, the nation of Israel was perpetually divided.

The seventh king of Israel was a man named Ahab. Evil to his core, his most fatal decision was his marriage to a foreign princess named Jezebel. She came from Sidon, and when she came, she brought her god, Baal. From the outset, her mission was simple: destroy the worship of God in Israel. Her method was also simple: add the worship of Baal. She did not seek to destroy the worship of God by demanding His removal but by suffocating His worship. The addition of Baal would lead to a slow demise of the steadfast worship of God. Her intent was that eventually the worship of God would die away completely.

As a remedy to this situation, God raised up the prophet Elijah. The quintessential prophet, Elijah confronted the error of the day, declaring extreme drought until he prophesied of rain. God had promised Israel extreme drought conditions if they gave themselves to idolatry, and Elijah was willing to believe that promise of God. For years, no rain fell. Finally, Elijah came out of hiding and proposed a challenge to Israel: Jezebel's priests of Baal versus God's prophet. They would offer a sacrifice to their deity, and whichever God answered with fire would win. They would worship Him.

But before they started their contest, Elijah questioned the people of Israel. "How long will you limp along between two opinions?" He saw a nation sick and hurting, limping along. Why were they limping? Two opinions . . . two gods . . . two targets of worship and affection.

This is the error Jezebel introduced—not raw sexual immorality and idol worship, but spiritual adultery. The church in Thyatira had become sick and diseased because they had added something. They had forgotten the majesty of the Son of God, in whom all the treasures of wisdom and knowledge are found.

They had added a thing, and that thing suffocated them. They limped along.

Historical Jezebel sought to destroy Israel by adding to it. Here, the spirit of Jezebel sought to destroy the church by adding to it. This is a deadly error that exists in our modern time. The church in Thyatira may have simply added worship of the patron deities to their worship of Christ—but they added, effectively killing themselves.

The modern church falls into this trap when we add additional missions to the gospel. If the church stands for a democratic republic with the same intensity as it stands for the gospel, eventually, the gospel will barely be heard. If the church stands for career development with the same intensity as it stands for the gospel, eventually, the gospel will barely be heard. If the church stands for acts of mercy with the same intensity as it stands for the gospel, eventually, the gospel will barely be heard.

Beyond these, of course, are the additions of blatant sins to the church. When sin is allowed to coexist with Christ, the love for Christ is eventually extinguished. For many believers, Baal—the love of money—has become their pursuit and devotion. This effectively kills a true devotion to Christ.

Again, Jezebel sought to secretly cripple Israel through simple addition, knowing the worship of God would eventually be subtracted from their midst. We must see this error for what it is, a limping along between two opinions. It kills us.

The question of Elijah stands out to our modern mind for the church in Thyatira: "How long will you go limping between two different opinions?" (1 Kings 18:21). The antidote to Jezebel is always Elijah. He forces the issue where she promotes compromise.

He demands allegiance where she offers multitudinous masters. But we must choose. Who will we serve? Who will we follow?

Solution

> I gave her time to repent, but she refuses to repent of her sexual immorality. Behold, I will throw her onto a sickbed, and those who commit adultery with her I will throw into great tribulation, unless they repent of her works, and I will strike her children dead. And all the churches will know that I am he who searches mind and heart, and I will give to each of you according to your works. (Revelation 2:21–23)

Here, Christ delivers the scolding disciplinary measures He will unleash upon the unrepentant in Thyatira. He had graciously given Jezebel time to repent. Soon, she and her followers would be thrown into great tribulation, struck dead after being thrown onto a sickbed. Their addition to Christ would not satisfy in the long run.

Only Christ could make such a bold statement. He indicates that Jezebel did not want to repent. Only Christ could know this. No man has this information, but Christ sees all. He knows with accuracy the hard-hearted unwillingness of Jezebel to repent. She did not want to. She refused.

In tabulating the coming judgment that would come upon them, Christ describes Himself as "He who searches minds and heart." Again, we go back to His description. He sees everything clearly; His eyes of fire penetrate even minds and hearts. Nothing is hidden from His sight. Before Christ, everything is naked and exposed.

Even now, Christ searches the hearts of His people. Have we tolerated Jezebel? Have we added to Christ? Are we guilty of adultery that is spiritual in nature? Have we given our minds or hearts over to that which has weakened the marital bond between Christ and us? Have we allowed fantasies that are unfitting for the Christian mind and heart? Christ searches our hearts, looking to root out the Jezebel within.

Exhortation

> But to the rest of you in Thyatira, who do not hold this teaching, who have not learned what some call the deep things of Satan, to you I say, I do not lay on you any other burden. Only hold fast what you have until I come. (Revelation 2:24–25)

There were still others in Thyatira who had not fallen prey to this deception. Not every church member had given themselves to Jezebel's doctrine. Many had remained steadfast. They had endured and did not hold to her teaching. They had "not learned what some call the deep things of Satan." This is likely Christ's commentary on the teaching of Jezebel. Her followers probably called her teaching "the deep things of God." Christ knows better; they are actually "the deep things of Satan."

This, of course, was the temptation in Thyatira—to believe Jezebel brought teachings of fabulous depth. Christ tells the church there, "I do not lay on you any other burden. Only hold fast what you have until I come." What did they have? What was the burden they already had? Christ. His gospel. Jesus Christ Himself is the true deep thing of God, but many in Thyatira had forgotten this.

But this is often the temptation. A distant relationship with Christ is a boring one, and this leads to a flirtation with lines of teaching and thought that go beyond Christ. We look for the "deeper things," forgetting that in Christ "are hidden all the treasures of wisdom and knowledge" (Colossians 2:3). Jesus Christ is the deep thing of God, no matter what the Jezebelists teach. The sooner a believer holds fast to that burden, the better.

Cling to Christ, for there is no other burden. When the emphasis of your Bible reading or study takes you away from Christ, beware. Continue to keep Him at the center of your thoughts. When the gospel becomes an afterthought, a danger exists. His message is the deep message. The entire Bible is about Him, for "the testimony of Jesus is the spirit of prophecy" (Revelation 19:10).

Promise
> The one who conquers and who keeps my works until the end, to him I will give authority over the nations, and he will rule them with a rod of iron, as when earthen pots are broken in pieces, even as I myself have received authority from my Father. And I will give him the morning star. He who has an ear, let him hear what the Spirit says to the churches. (Revelation 2:26–29)

To the believers in Thyatira came Christ's eternal promise. He did this in every letter for every believer. He calls them conquerors . . . overcomers. Various eternal riches await the church; here, the emphasis is on the rule of Christ with a rod of iron. They would partake in His authority over the nations and that rod of iron. This promise has roots in Psalm 2: "You shall break them with a rod of iron and dash them in pieces like a potter's vessel" (Psalm 2:9).

Jesus Christ has been promised "the throne of His father David" (Luke 1:32). He "will be king over all the earth" (Zechariah 14:9). Jesus told His disciples they would sit enthroned with
Him once He sat on David's reestablished earthly throne: "Truly,
I say to you, in the new world, when the Son of Man will sit on
his glorious throne, you who have followed me will also sit on
twelve thrones, judging the twelve tribes of Israel" (Matthew
19:28). Twelve thrones for twelve disciples, seated along with
Christ. But when will this be? When Jesus is about to ascend, the
disciples ask, "Lord, will you at this time restore the kingdom
to Israel?" (Acts 1:6). He responds by telling them, "It is not for
you to know times and seasons that the Father has fixed by his
own authority" (Acts 1:7). He does not rebuke the idea of Israel's
restoration but rather, the idea that they would know the timing.
They were not to know the timing, but the day will still come.

Near the end of Revelation, John writes:

> Then I saw an angel coming down from heaven, hold-
> ing in his hand the key to the bottomless pit and a great
> chain. And he seized the dragon, that ancient serpent,
> who is the devil and Satan, and bound him for a thou-
> sand years, and threw him into the pit, and shut it and
> sealed it over him, so that he might not deceive the na-
> tions any longer, until the thousand years were ended.
> After that, he must be released for a little while. Then I
> saw thrones, and seated on them were those to whom
> the authority to judge was committed. Also, I saw the
> souls of those who had been beheaded for the testi-
> mony of Jesus and for the word of God, and those who
> had not worshiped the beast or its image and had not
> received its mark on their foreheads or their hands.
> They came to life and reigned with Christ for a thou-
> sand years. The rest of the dead did not come to life

until the thousand years were ended. This is the first
resurrection. Blessed and holy is the one who shares
in the first resurrection! Over such the second death
has no power, but they will be priests of God and of
Christ, and they will reign with him for a thousand
years. (Revelation 20:1–6).

Notice the thousand years, the thrones, the resurrection, and the
reign with Christ. Jesus tells the remnant church in Thyatira they
will partake in that glorious age. After His return, He will re-
establish Israel and rule this world for a thousand years. What
follows will be a melting away of this earth (2 Peter 3:10) and
new heavens and new earth (Revelation 21–22). This hope isn't
universally held by the modern church, nor is it a view worth di-
viding over, but it seems to be the hope Christ gave the Thyatiran
believers.

Thyatira would also receive Christ, "the morning star" (see Revelation 22:16). They may have been in darkness now, but they
would live in His bright illumination then. Right now we might
be perplexed (2 Corinthians 4:8), but the day of light will come.
The Morning Star will be ours.

"But for you who fear my name, the sun of righteousness shall
rise with healing in its wings. You shall go out leaping like calves
from the stall." (Malachi 4:2)

CHAPTER 6

Sardis

Samuel the prophet was on a mission: get to Jesse's house and anoint his son as the next king of Israel—Saul's replacement. Upon arrival, Jesse gathered his sons and the feast began. When Samuel saw Jesse's oldest son, he thought, "Surely the Lord's anointed is before him" (1 Samuel 16:6). But it was not so. God did not accept him or the next six brothers for the task.

After inquiring if there was another absent son, Jesse told Samuel there was the youngest, David. He was tending the sheep and had not received an invitation to the day's festivities. "We will not sit down till he comes here," was Samuel's reply (1 Samuel 16:11).

David came, and the rest is history. But recall Samuel's encounter with the oldest son, Eliab. God had said, "Do not look on his appearance or the height of his stature, because I have rejected him. For the Lord sees not as man sees: man looks on the outward appearance, but the Lord looks on the heart" (1 Samuel 16:7).

God looks on the heart. This was the lesson Samuel, Jesse's family, and all of Israel needed to learn. When they selected Saul, they chose the tallest and the most handsome. But this was not the plan or heart of God—He chose differently. All man can see is the outward, but God sees the heart.

The example of David, Eliab, and Samuel helps us in our understanding of the letter of Jesus to the church in Sardis. From outward appearances they were alive, but Christ saw the internal, calling them dead. As with David and Eliab, God saw more than man could see.

"You have the reputation of being alive, but you are dead" (Revelation 3:1). Sardis was dead; this is Christ's assessment. No one else could make this assessment with accuracy. Who are we to pass judgment on the servant of another? We don't know the internal workings of a man's heart, but Christ sees the internal workings of the entire church in Sardis and rebukes it swiftly.

Fortunately for Sardis, and for us, Christ immediately gives Sardis directions. He teaches them how to get out of deadness. They didn't have to remain dead. Death was not their destiny. The mere presence of these directions is grace. The same Jesus Christ who resurrected from the grave can resurrect Sardis from theirs.

So this letter will encourage us to strive for true life in Christ's estimation. This life is accomplished by staying awake, strengthening what remains, and completing our works.

Description of Sardis

Sardis was a wealthy city at the time of John, but it wasn't the wealth of hard labor. It was easy money, as the gold-bearing Pactolus River that ran through Sardis had brought prosperity to many. This affluence led to luxury, and famous woven fabrics were bought and sold there. And, as the outermost destination on the royal road, Sardis was an important trade outpost. When modern coinage was introduced to Asia Minor, it was Sardis that introduced it; the city was that prosperous.

Sardis was a place of commerce, a place where billionaires like history's famous Croesus resided. As with many wealthy populaces, it would be easy for the people of Sardis to lack a hunger for God, having been lulled to sleep by ease. The church of Sardis would be no different. They, too, could fall prey to this age-old trap of the enemy.

Sardis was also a defensible city. With many cliffs and high places, they were apparently in a good strategic military position. This defensibility of the town played an unfortunate role in their history. Twice, infamously, they had been overtaken in the night due to their high confidence in their military positioning.

Once, in 549 BC, the previously mentioned Croesus had fled from King Cyrus to the city of Sardis. Thinking himself safe, Croesus did not stay on alert. Cyrus's forces scaled the cliffs in the darkness of night, ultimately defeating Croesus. And again, in 214 BC, Antiochus repeated Cyrus's feat, stealing into the city in the dead of night and conquering it. These two episodes lingered in the minds of every citizen in Sardis, having become part of the lore of the town.

It is easy to see how this would play into the letter of Christ to the church there. They had a reputation for life but were dead, and Jesus tells them to wake up. As in Sardis's ancient history, the best remedy would be an alertness. Don't grow overconfident in your lofty position. Christ wants an awake church.

Spiritual deadness cannot be remedied without the Holy Spirit making you alive. The church in Sardis was also under this rule. They needed the Holy Spirit to revive them.

Description of Jesus

> And to the angel of the church in Sardis write: "The words of him who has the seven spirits of God and the seven stars." (Revelation 3:1).

Fortunately, Christ is the One "who has the seven spirits of God." This turn of phrase does not mean there are seven Holy Spirits, but that God pours out the fullness of His Spirit. In the Bible, seven is the number of completion, like in the full seven-day week humanity generally practices.

Consider this passage in Isaiah 11, where the singular Holy Spirit is described in seven ways: "There shall come forth a shoot from the stump of Jesse, and a branch from his roots shall bear fruit. And the Spirit of the Lord shall rest upon him, the Spirit of wisdom and understanding, the Spirit of counsel and might, the Spirit of knowledge and the fear of the Lord" (Isaiah 11:1–2).

So it seems Jesus has the fullness of the Spirit to offer the dead church in Sardis. Perhaps they were in need of new birth, or perhaps they were in need of reviving. Whatever the cause, Paul would have asked this church, "Did you receive the Holy Spirit when you believed?" (Acts 19:2).

In Luke 11, Jesus teaches us, as His people, about prayer to the Father. Christ has won that Father-child relationship for us with God the Father. In this chapter, he tells us to ask, seek, and knock before the Father, who gives good gifts. Earthly fathers have figured out how to give bread and fish, not snakes and scorpions; this is a reflection of the heavenly Father. Then Jesus says, "the heavenly Father [will] give the Holy Spirit to those who ask Him" (Luke 11:13).

The church in Sardis needed to come alive by the Spirit. Do you? We always need His fresh supply and life, His living water flowing from our hearts. Feed the Spirit. To feed the flesh leads to corruption and death, but to feed the Spirit leads to life. Allow the Spirit within to grow stronger and stronger, bringing the flesh into submission. Sardis needed the Spirit and so do we.

Correction

> I know your works. You have the reputation of being
> alive, but you are dead. (Revelation 3:1)

This statement from Christ stops us dead in our tracks. It is searching, loud, and impossible to misunderstand. He was not diluting his words for Sardis; they came full strength out of His mouth. He told them, "People think you are alive, but you are dead." Let us consider this.

There is, of course, such a thing as a dead church. Perhaps you have knowingly visited one—a church where the form and function are still there, but it is a hollow experience. Perhaps the church has dwindled to the point there is no new life, no conversions, no youth. Maybe you, with your own eyes, can easily discern, "This church seems to be dead."

In his commentary on the book of Revelation, Charles Swindoll tells of five marks of a dead church: they worship their past, they are inflexible and resistant to change, they have lazy leadership, they neglect the next generation, and they lack evangelistic zeal. All of these are searching statements, an excellent metric for church health, and I refer to them often. But I do not think they accurately describe the church in Sardis.

Sardis wasn't a dead church that everyone knew to be dead; actually, everyone thought it was alive. There weren't twenty-five gray-haired saints sitting in a thousand-seat auditorium, reminiscing about the good old days of their church. No, Sardis didn't have the reputation of being dead, but of being alive. Their auditorium was full. But Christ saw something a man could not see.

Sardis wasn't in outward decay but inward decay. God's presence wasn't there, but they ticked on ahead as if nothing had happened. Like the Pharisees, they looked clean and whitewashed on the outside but were filthy and dead on the inside (Matthew 23:25–39).

They likely had all the externals of organization and gatherings and music and giving and prayers. The signs of life were all there externally, but they were absent internally.

An athlete could understand this concept. Take a good marathoner and give him a few years off from running. Have him eat well during his time off, perhaps even have him lift weights and stay reasonably fit. Then, after years without running, bring him out to a marathon. Dress him up and have him look the part. You might bet he'd perform well, but he won't, because his internal fitness is gone. He cannot run as he used to. Externally he might not look that different, but his heart cannot do what it used to. His fitness for running has departed, and he must build it up again.

None of us wants this. No one ever wants externals only. No one wants to sing only if it is shallow, without thought, and emotionless. No one wants to give as long as there is no thought to what the money might accomplish or the eternal friends it might make. And no one wants to pray merely as a vain repetition or recitation . . . a robotic mumbling of thought.

No! We want something real. We want the externals to operate as vehicles to drive us into the presence of God. We want
the externals to stir up the internals. We want songs to lead us
to God's glorification. We want gifts to lead us to dependence
upon Him. We want prayers to shape our attitudes and perspectives. We want something real, true, inward. We will not settle
for mere externals.

But this church in Sardis had done just that. The externals existed, but the internals were lacking. Like the self-indulgent widow
of 1 Timothy 5, they were dead while they lived (1 Timothy 5:6).
This is most unattractive, repugnant, and unwanted.

Solution

> Wake up, and strengthen what remains and is about to
> die, for I have not found your works complete in the
> sight of my God. Remember, then, what you received
> and heard. Keep it, and repent. If you will not wake up,
> I will come like a thief, and you will not know at what
> hour I will come against you. (Revelation 3:2–3)

Is not all hope lost for the Sardis church? Are they not dead? Various illnesses have remedies, but there is no medicine for death . .
. unless Christ is your Lord. He is the firstborn from the dead, the
resurrected Son of God. Since He resurrected, we can resurrect.
Life was possible for Sardis because Christ had made it possible.

What is His first instruction to them in their deadness? Wake up.
Keep awake. Be on guard.

Remember their city's history? Through sleep they had been defeated. Christ tells the church there not to fall to the same fate. Instead, wake up. Be alert.

Alertness is the calling of every Christian. Paul said, "The hour has come for you to wake from sleep" (Romans 13:11). Again he writes, "Awake, O sleeper, and arise from the dead, and Christ will shine on you" (Ephesians 5:14). Peter told the church to "be sober-minded; be watchful" (1 Peter 5:8). Christ told us to "be on guard, keep awake" (Mark 13:33). In various ways and for various reasons, believers are to be awake before God.

For Sardis, this would have meant they would arise from their self-confidence. It had turned into overconfidence. They thought their reputation was accurate, that they were alive. They had mistakenly believed their own press—what others had said of them. To wake up, they had to take the estimations of man and throw them out, for it is only Christ's evaluation that matters.

Is this not helpful in an era where we look at the external metrics of a church's life and judge its health?

Jesus then introduces the next step, for it would not have been sufficient for them only to wake up. "And strengthen what remains and is about to die, for I have not found your works complete in the sight of my God." They next needed to strengthen something. He describes that something as that which "remains and is about to die." What are these things that remain? What was about to die?

Well, He next says, "For I have not found your works complete in the sight of my God." These are the remaining things: their works. All the externals that made people think they were alive were incomplete before God. They were there...but they were incomplete, and now they were in need of strengthening.

So it seems Jesus is telling this church in Sardis to take their already-existent works and breathe some life into them. They attended church services, we would imagine, but now they needed to actually be present in their attendance. They prayed words, but now they were actually to pray in the Spirit. They gave, but now they were actually to give from their hearts. The heart was to be put into actions in all areas.

The Bible speaks of various Israelite kings in a number of ways. Of King Amaziah it says, "He did what was right in the eyes of the Lord, yet not with a whole heart" (2 Chronicles 25:2). A whole heart is what Sardis needed. They were doing right in the eyes of the Lord, but now they needed a whole heart in doing those works. Their practices needed to be strengthened in some timeless issues.

Worship. When Sardis sang their psalms and hymns and spiritual songs, they needed to put emotion and thought and meaning into their singing. The routines of corporate worship can become dead to us as well...but the Spirit awaits. He is ready to lift our hearts from the mundane and into the heavens. In the song, He wants to give us a glimpse of the throne of God. "Strengthen what remains."

Giving. When Sardis gave their tithes and offerings and gifts, they needed to put their hearts and minds and souls into the giving. When we give, we must think of the effect: God's Word is given more of a platform, and God's Word is the necessary cure for the spiritual cancers that ail humanity. God's spiritual people are helped in the physical realm through our generosity. Our own hearts are set free from captivity to the slave masters of covetousness and greed. The Spirit wants to use our financial gifts to transform the world and also to transform us. "Strengthen what remains."

Service. When the people of Sardis volunteered and helped and spoke, they needed to put their whole beings into the process. Likewise, are we not tempted to serve in body but not in spirit? Do we not fall prey to a laziness of mind and heart in our service, going through the motions? Stephen and Philip care for the daily distribution to the widows in the early Jerusalem church. It was not glamorous. But because they did it with fervency, life, and zeal, new doors were opened to them. Half-heartedness in our service will not do. "Strengthen what remains."

Prayer. When Sardis interceded and petitioned, they needed to get their hearts and minds and bodies unlocked for the work. Do we not also utter prayers that are void of life? They might even have emotion, but the emotion isn't genuine. Christ looks for something real—a true heart before Him. "Strengthen what remains."

In every element of life, the believers in Sardis needed to wake up and strengthen what remained. We are called to do the same.

Jesus then tells them to "remember, then, what you received and heard. Keep it, and repent." Sardis had wandered from the gospel they had received and heard. Perhaps this is where their death had come from. The gospel had been heard, and the gospel had been received, but they had begun to drift from it—perhaps not in disbelief, but due to a lack of emphasis or attention. They had stopped thinking of Christ and His glorious cross. They had ceased meditating on the position Christ had won for them. They had drifted, and this deviation had begun to kill them to the point that Christ called them dead.

Is this not often the case with the dead church? The outward forms are often found in the dead church. Their doctrine might even be in order, but the life is gone because the gospel is gone, underemphasized, and never celebrated. Get back to the central themes of Christianity. Love them. Celebrate them. Rejoice over them. Find a church and believers who will do likewise.

Promise

> Yet you have still a few names in Sardis, people who have not soiled their garments, and they will walk with me in white, for they are worthy. (Revelation 3:4).

Christ sees a "few names in Sardis" who have not "soiled their garments." He knows His sheep. He sees the faithful remnant in Sardis. Even in this dead church, there were still some pockets of life. These folks would walk with Christ in white, for they had not dirtied their garments.

John had written in 1 John 1:7: "But if we walk in the light, as he is in the light, we have fellowship with one another, and the blood of Jesus his Son cleanses us from all sin." To walk in the light means experiential fellowship with Christ. These believers in Sardis would experience that fellowship.

Christ has set us free that we might enjoy Him. This enjoyment is not for eternity only, but for today. Everlasting life begins now. Some in Sardis had refused to muddy their lives with a world-liness that would keep them from a practical enjoyment of the Christ of heaven. Their experience was that of the enjoyment of Christ.

Today, the church needs to experience depth with Christ. We are an overstimulated culture. Certainly, God has given creation to enjoy, but Christ is our deepest enjoyment. We enjoy creation with Christ and through Christ. To soil ourselves with sin keeps us from the deep enjoyment of Christ that some in Sardis experienced. "Come now, let us reason together, says the Lord: though your sins are like scarlet, they shall be as white as snow; though they are red like crimson, they shall become like wool." (Isaiah 1:18). These clean garments help us walk in cleanness. Like Noah and Enoch, we have the blessing of being remade to walk with God (Genesis 5:22, 6:9).

> The one who conquers will be clothed thus in white garments, and I will never blot his name out of the book of life. I will confess his name before my Father and before his angels. He who has an ear, let him hear what the Spirit says to the churches. (Revelation 3:5–6)

Again, we have the promise to the conquerors, the believers, the overcomers. All the promises to the conqueror are eternal in nature. These are promises for believers. Here, Christ highlights the security of the believer: "I will never blot his name out of the book of life." This indicates the eternal security of the believer. Once the name is in, it is in. It cannot be blotted out; it is permanent and secure, and Christ exhorts them to enjoy this reality.

We thirst for acceptance and security. In an ever-shifting world, it's hard to find a home, but Christ provides that secure home for His people. "I will confess his name before my Father and before His angels," He says. He will confess His people to the Father at His throne. Is this not our deep need—the acceptance of God? The Sardis believers could rest knowing of their secure position in Christ. What joy this would bring them—and us, too!

> Truly, truly, I say to you, whoever hears my word and
> believes him who sent me has eternal life. He does not
> come into judgment, but has passed from death to life.
> (John 5:24)

The church in Sardis serves as a case study of a dead church. But life was possible. They had to wake up, and anyone spiritually dead, going through the motions, must wake up. "Strengthen that which remains."

Remember, Christ sees not as man sees. He sees the truth. Like Sardis, we could have a reputation for life, but the Lord knows if there is death in us. But by His resurrection power and the strength of the Spirit He provides, we can come back into the glorious life He's called us to.

CHAPTER 7

Philadelphia

One aim of the Christian is to leave earth with as few regrets as possible. Today we walk by faith, not by sight, but the day is coming when the order will be reversed. One day we will walk by sight, not faith. We will see God quite visibly. In our new glorified bodies, we will experience Him completely, fully. Faith will give way to sight. When that day will come . . . no man knows, but we do know we want to enter into it with as few regrets as possible.

This life is our one chance to walk by faith. For all the pains this life presents us, faith is its unique opportunity.

In our study of the seven letters, we have seen the problems and difficulties in various churches. We've also read words of commendation from Christ. He rejoices over some of what He observes and mourns over other elements. The job of the modern reader and church, of course, is to discern the difference and revive that which is in need of reviving within us.

As we come to the church in Philadelphia, we discover a church Christ thought highly of. They might not have been the dynamo that the church in Ephesus had been, but they had some fruit, an opportunity, and a little strength to go with it. The Philadelphian church had an opportunity—an open door—directly from Christ. With the little strength they possessed, they were to walk through the doors Christ had given them. They were to live without regrets. They were to live a life of faith.

Description of Philadelphia

The city of Philadelphia was intended to be a cultural outpost of Greek culture, language, and thought. Rome did not have military designs for her. She would not use brute strength to subdue the lesser-known regions beyond. No, Philadelphia was to be an outpost not of Rome's intimidating military might, but of culture and language. It was to be, in a sense, an evangelistic herald of the Greek way of life.

The spread of Roman culture through Philadelphia would have implications for the church there. Christ will give them their own open door, their own opportunity. They weren't to operate as Rome's ambassadors but as ambassadors for Christ. They were to bring news of a better kingdom to the regions beyond. Every place Rome wanted to subdue with Greek culture, Christ wanted His church to subdue with His kingdom.

Additionally, Philadelphia had a history of severe earthquakes. At various moments in their past, the people of the city would have to leave Philadelphia due to the severity of the damage caused by a new tremor. Pillars in different temples would stand, but much of the city would have to be rebuilt.

This familiarity with rebuilding would stand out to the church in Philadelphia. Later, Christ will comfort them with eternity, that they would be made into pillars in the temple of God, never to depart. They were acquainted with flight from danger. They had lived in insecurity. And in a world of insecurity, the Philadel-phian church was promised future security in Christ with God.

Description of Jesus

> And to the angel of the church in Philadelphia write: "The words of the holy one, the true one, who has the key of David, who opens and no one will shut, who shuts and no one opens." (Revelation 3:7)

In every letter, as we've seen, Christ describes Himself. His description is His prescription, for the church needs more of Christ. He was their answer, and He is ours. For this church, He held out His holy and genuine nature, followed by a longer statement regarding "the key of David." With that key, he would open, and no one would shut. He would shut, and no one would open.

The first thing to note is that this is a direct quote of Isaiah 22:22. Jesus lifts a passage from Isaiah's prophecies to talk of His current ministry. Going back to the Isaiah passage reveals some helpful details to us.

There, a man named Shebna operates as the steward of the king's palace. The steward ran the home. He possessed the master key to the entire residence, so every room was accessible to him. In the Isaiah prophecy, Shebna is rebuked. God then promises to replace him with a man named Eliakim. It was he who would have the key of David to open and shut.

In the Isaiah 22 passage, Shebna is removed, and Eliakim is promoted. But here in Revelation, Christ claims the ultimate position. He, not Eliakim, now has the key of David. He now opens, and no one shuts; He now shuts, and no one opens. He has the keys.

Perhaps the church of Philadelphia was to consider this particular work and ministry of Christ in their cultural context. We are to do the same. Perhaps we would be helped to imagine a palace with many rooms. Allow each room to represent various individuals, people groups, churches, states, or nations. Now, imagine Christ as the One with the master key to unlock each room—each person, people group, church, state, or country. Christ is the One who must access these opportunities for us.

Think of your region of the world. Where are the challenging places, the hard-to-get-to regions or peoples? Christ has the key. We must turn to Him for the open door.

In the book of Zechariah, there was a struggle. Some Jews had been allowed to return to Jerusalem to rebuild the temple, but the work was slow going. In the slog, the leaders grew discouraged with the enormity of the task. Zerubbabel was the governor at the time and one of the discouraged leaders. The Lord spoke to him through Zechariah: "Not by might, nor by power, but by My Spirit" (Zechariah 4:6). It would not be their strategy or ingenuity that would bring about the victory, but the Spirit of God.

Our modern mind ought to be shaped by these ancient revelations. Christ has the key. He is the steward who opens the doors of opportunity to His church. We must walk through the doors, but we must first understand He is the giver of the opportunity itself. Make no mistake—He has given us a great opportunity. He opens doors.

Praise

> I know your works. Behold, I have set before you an
> open door, which no one is able to shut. I know that

you have but little power, and yet you have kept my
word and have not denied my name. (Revelation 3:8)

Christ then tells this church they are a church of opportunity. "I
have set before you an open door," He says. The door was firmly
opened, and no one could shut it.

They had a missionary opportunity from Christ opened up for
them. No longer were they to operate as cultural missionaries for
Rome; they now belonged to Christ.

In our modern world, it is imperative for the Christian to sort out
his citizenship. We are dual citizens of sorts—first of our nation,
but primarily of heaven. Our preeminent citizenship is that of
heaven. The church in Philippi had to hear this, for they lived in a
proud Roman colony. The Philippian soil was considered Rome's
soil. Their connection to Rome could have dulled their fire, so
Paul was sure to remind them, "Your citizenship is in heaven"
(Philippians 3:20).

What comes from your mouth? What culture and customs are
you promoting? Are you a stronger evangel of your earthly nation than your heavenly one? The Philadelphian church, to enter
the doors Christ had opened for them, had to first set aside their
previous mission from Rome. At the very least, they had to make
it a distant second.

But what are we to make of this open door Christ has given
them? Quite often, our first response when reading of an open
door is to consider the smoothest path. In our minds, that must
be the open door. But the way of the cross was far from the most
effortless path, and our open doors will likewise be difficult at
times. Paul spoke to the church in Corinth about a "wide door for
effective work" being opened to him, but he added, "and there

are many adversaries" (I Corinthians 16:9). In other words, Paul saw a major opportunity for the Lord in front of him, but it was filled with adversaries. The adversaries' presence didn't mean the door was closed. If anything, they confirmed it was a door from the Lord.

No, the smooth path is not the door of Christ. It is the broad and easy way that leads to destruction. It is the narrow gate and the difficult way that leads to life. Often, this is the case with the opportunities God gives us in working for Christ. As they say, nothing worth doing is easy. Christ's call is no different.

We can only imagine the doors Christ opened for the church of Philadelphia. We can, however, attempt to discern the doors Christ has opened for us. Christ gives us daily opportunities to share the gospel. We are to testify of His gospel and grace in our lives, and the open doors for this testimony are numerous. Here are a few open doors I believe Christ has given the modern church:

Emotional health. Jesus Christ is a redeemer—this includes the realm of the inner man. As we allow Christ to work in us, a mental and emotional health will grow within us. Perfection will not be ours, but positive growth will be.

Contentment. Paul spoke to the Philippians of having learned the secret of contentment. The man had become able to find satisfaction in any condition of life, whether abased or abounding. When Christ grows us to a less worried, less covetous, less anxious existence, the results become obvious to those around us. This can be an open door for the gospel.

Familial health. Various societies war against biblical marriage and, therefore, family structure. The heart provides the motives for their belief systems, and the heart often wants a sexually un-tethered life. Committed male-female marital relations are re-jected, giving way to anything and everything else. The concept, we are told, is that the biblical family structure is antiquated and unscientific. Yet a redeemed family is a beacon of hope in a sea of despair. A husband who lovingly leads his family, serving them well, is a fresh wind of encouragement. A wife who respects her husband intensely, gladly enjoying his role in her life, is new. And when children under their care show the obvious benefits of this structure, the results are striking. The contrast to the broken and hurtful experiences of so many could not be starker. This health can be an open door for the gospel.

Personal experiences with Christ. Christianity is intellectual and cerebral, but it is also highly experiential. The Scriptures teach that the Holy Spirit comes to live inside of us . . . that we are to pray and fast . . . that we are to walk with God, enjoying fellowship with Him. We experience the gifts of the Spirit. We read and study the Bible, which teaches us it is living and power-ful—the book is alive! This leads us to various tangible and real experiences with God. The world seems infatuated with the su-pernatural. It seems they understand that there must be more to life than what they see and know. People thirst for encounters with the divine, and the devil is perniciously prepared to indulge them. But the Christ follower has true and real experiences to draw from. Walking in the Spirit, he personally experiences the grace of God. These experiences can be an open door for the gospel.

God's great grace. In all of this, there is the grace of God. Our emotional health, family structures, and personal experiences may be lacking, but God's love remains. This, of course, is the loud message of Christ: "Come to me, all who labor and are and heavy laden, and I will give you rest" (Matthew 11:28). In a world filled with works-based religiosity, the gospel is a fresh breath of God's great grace. This grace is an open door for the gospel.

So the church in Philadelphia was a church with an open door. We would do well to pray regarding the open doors Christ has given to us. We would do well to ask for more. "At the same time, pray also for us, that God may open to us a door for the word, to declare the mystery of Christ" (Colossians 4:3).

The next element of this letter is beautiful: "I know that you have but little power, and yet you have kept my word and have not denied my name." Christ saw the limited strength of the Philadelphian church and praised them for it. Their weakness was called "little power" by the Lord, yet He exalts them for the strength they did have.

Small strength ought to create a powerful dependence on the Lord. This is how Paul the Apostle processed his weaknesses. At a crisis point in life, he asked the Lord to relieve him of a "thorn" that buffeted him. His pain was palpable. Still, Christ announced the thorn would remain; the pain would last. God's grace was sufficient for Paul, and His strength was made perfect in Paul's weakness. In response, Paul decided thus: "Therefore I will boast all the more gladly of my weakness, so that the power of Christ may rest upon me. For the sake of Christ, then, I am content with weaknesses, insults, hardships, persecutions, and calamities. For when I am weak, then I am strong" (2 Corinthians 12:9–10).

The small strength in Philadelphia likely helped them do a strong work for God. When we feel strong, we are tempted to the Laodicean error of self-sufficiency, but a feeling of weakness can create a dependence that is the pathway to power. Think of the victorious moments in Israel's history. They had multitudinous stories of God's power, but the pathway in each story was eerily similar. God trod the same path of man's weakness to manifest His greatness. Abraham and Sarah were too aged to have a child, yet God gave them one. Israel was too weak to defeat Egypt, yet God did it for them. They had no army with which to overflow the walled city of Jericho, yet God's might toppled the walls. Over and over again God manifested His strength in the smallness of man.

God is the same today. The Philadelphian church had tiny strength, yet God would work mightily through them. They were the church of the open door. The modern church might feel this smallness of strength, but that should not dissipate their view of the open door from Christ. It remains. Let the Red Sea pathway or Jericho's defeat or Gideon's army or Goliath's fall model the power of God for today. The same strength remains for the church today.

If you find yourself in a place of weakness or smallness . . . rejoice! It is there His power might be made manifest in your life. He cannot work in our strength, for it cancels out His power. He looks for the humble, the dependent, the desperate. Think about it; you know it to be true. We will hardly pray when we feel strong, but in weakness, we cry to God. He craves this brand of dependence. Lean upon Him. With the little strength of the Philadelphian church, go! The open doors are there, and His Spirit waits to empower us, but now we must move through the door.

Promises

> Behold, I will make those of the synagogue of Satan who say that they are Jews and are not, but lie—behold, I will make them come and bow down before your feet, and they will learn that I have loved you. (Revelation 3:9)

Apparently, the church in Philadelphia suffered similar pressure to the Smyrna church (Revelation 2:9). Not every Jew is seen this way, for the early church was predominantly Jewish, and all her apostles certainly were Jewish. Our Messiah is Jewish! But the Jewish contingent in Philadelphia and Smyrna had somehow slandered and persecuted the churches in those places. Perhaps it was more intense in Smyrna, but it was similar in Philadelphia.

But who pressured the church in Philadelphia is less important than the fact that they were pressured. The door in front of them was not without adversaries, and here Christ lists them. Jesus promises something powerful to the Philadelphians. A day would come when he would "make them come and bow down before your feet." This speaks of a day when the truth is acknowledged by all, but with a different emphasis than we might be used to. Famous are the verses that speak of every knee bowing and every tongue confessing that Christ is Lord (Isaiah 45:23, Romans 14:11, Philippians 2:10). This day will come, but this isn't the point Christ makes to the Philadelphians. To them, He says their persecutors would bow before them, not Him. He quotes from Isaiah 60:14:"The sons of those who afflicted you shall come bending low to you, and all who despised you shall bow down at your feet" (Isaiah 60:14). The quote is astounding. Initially, it speaks of Gentiles bowing before Jews, but here Christ uses it to suggest Jewish persecutors bowing before a predominantly Gentile church.

There was more, however. "And they will learn that I have loved you." This statement is tender . . . beautiful. The day would come when this hardworking missionary church would finish their course. Then, their persecutors would know of Christ's love toward them. Anyone who has ever endured a marathon knows of the joy of the finish line, and this finish line is of the sweetest kind, for the love of Christ is proved there. They were loved all along. Persecuted, with small strength and open doors, but loved.

Should not the love and admiration of Christ be a stronger motivation to the modern heart? He sits on His eternal throne awaiting our arrival. This life here is minuscule in comparison to the life there. Life now is temporary, but life beyond is everlasting, eternal, unending. Perhaps the hatred of a persecutor hurts now, but the love of Christ will heal then, and the experience of it will be unending. Let us tap into this glorious love now, while here, while operating through the open doors Christ has given us.

> Because you have kept my word about patient endurance, I will keep you from the hour of trial that is coming on the whole world, to try those who dwell on the earth. I am coming soon. Hold fast what you have, so that no one may seize your crown. (Revelation 3:10–11)

The Philadelphian church, as the true church does, would escape the great tribulation coming upon the entire world. This statement has fostered great debate, but consider the hope it would have given the Philadelphian believers. The open door might be arduous, but not in comparison to the love of Christ and the coming hour of trial. They would get the love, not the trial. Naturally, the church often endures trials, but the wrath of God is no more for His church. It was satisfied at the cross. The Philadelphian believers would escape it.

Given the hope of His soon return, they were exhorted to hold fast to what they had, so that no one would seize their crown. What they had has already been detailed by Christ. They had an open door. They had a little strength. They had faithfulness to Christ. These were theirs, and they were not to let them go. Hold fast to them, Christ taught. There was a reward for them, and it was coming, but they had to hold fast, making sure no one took their crown.

I find often I am the stealer of my own crown. I tend to hinder my walk. The reward of serving Christ is rich, but I frequently hijack that service with a desire for praise or ease or sin. So we must be on guard. As Proverbs 4:23 states, "Keep your heart with all vigilance, for from it flow the springs of life." Guard that heart; don't let yourself lose sight of the crown.

> The one who conquers, I will make him a pillar in the temple of my God. Never shall he go out of it, and I will write on him the name of my God, and the name of the city of my God, the new Jerusalem, which comes down from my God out of heaven, and my own new name. He who has an ear, let him hear what the Spirit says to the churches. (Revelation 3:12–13)

This closing promise to believers would have stood out as an immense blessing to the Philadelphian church. First, they would be pillars in the temple of God. There were actual pillars in Israel's temple. One was named after Boaz, Solomon's great-great grandfather. Another was named after Jachin, the first high priest in Solomon's temple. The Philadelphian church was accustomed to displacement due to earthquakes, so to hear they'd be a pillar in God's eternal home would stand as a blessing. Christ said, "Never shall he go out of it." The promise could not be more fitting.

Christ offered a permanent place in His heaven to the church in Philadelphia. For a people who lived under the fear of displacement, this promise stood out as an immense blessing. Eternally, they would stand secure in Him, without fear of evacuation, without uncertainty.

Do we not today have a strong desire for this certain standing? Aren't we craving this kind of security? This brand of permanency? Christ will give the Philadelphian church—and us—a new name and a new place—permanency before Him.

This security is important for people on Christ's mission. We feel our strength is small, but Christ has given an open door. As we move through the door He's given, we feel our smallness. We wonder if we are making much of a difference at all. We wonder where our place is. Here, Christ tells them and us that our place is wrapped up in and with Him eternally.

Anyone who has ever sat with a small yet faithful group of believers knows the power of this letter to the Philadelphian church. In nations where the church is the rather extreme minority, this letter is a treasure. The open door, the keys, the little strength— all of it brings encouragement to the soul of the Philadelphia-like church. Even with their smallness, they are loved in the sight of Christ and given an opportunity by Him. Let us hear the Spirit well.

CHAPTER 8

Laodicea

During a solar eclipse, the sun is obscured by the moon. Beautiful and rare, the solar eclipse obstructs our view of the sun. The Laodicean church had done the same, but it was not a beautiful thing; they'd sabotaged the glorious light of Christ. The church is meant to be the light of the world; Jesus even called us "the light of the world" (Matthew 5:14). These letters testify to the church's light-bearing mission, as we see Jesus walking among the lampstands. The church is to illuminate the world. But the Laodicean church was what Christ called "lukewarm," and lukewarmness never illuminates anything. Lukewarmness is a plague, a cancer that kills the beautiful light of Christ.

Paul taught that we are ambassadors for Christ (2 Corinthians 5:20). To be His ambassadors means we are representatives of Jesus Christ. His positions, mood, feelings, and thoughts are to be represented to the world by His people. This is part of our light-bearing work and ministry. But if the Laodicean people had looked to the Laodicean church to discern God's attitude, they would have seen indifference. Laodicea is the church of the shoulder shrug, for they were uncaring. They gave the impression that Christ is careless.

Laodicea had no word of praise; they were that far gone. Christ could find something praiseworthy in nearly every city—even in churches embedded in profound error. But He could not abide the Laodicean lukewarmness. The taste of it was repulsive to Him. So repulsive, in fact, He warned of vomiting them from His mouth.

So the Laodicean letter has a severity to it. Many modern believers already know this. Perhaps you began reading this book with a preconceived understanding that you do not want to be the Laodicean believer. The situation there was dire, and Christ pointed it out. Perhaps this letter stands out to you as one of great despair.

Let it not be so. The mere presence of this letter gives us hope. Yes, it is the harshest of the letters, but the hope in it is astounding. A church this dysfunctional, this prideful, this distasteful, had the hope of restoration by Christ. The mere presence of the letter shows He isn't done with them. But then the contents of the letter show us a way forward. No, this is not a hopeless letter, but a hopeful note for every believer who has ever battled the lukewarm tepidness found in the Laodicean church.

Have you ever felt a carelessness wash over your heart? Have you ever sensed a low interest in the things of God, yet without a full rebellion against His name? Have you ever been tempted to play the middle ground, neither hot nor cold for Christ? It is one of the most common temptations known to man. The enemy of our souls is happy to render us "Laodicean." He would love to make us tepid, lukewarm, and uncaring. This temptation always lies at the door, but we must rule over it. Christ seems to provide four means of overcoming lukewarmness. Let us consider them.

Description of Laodicea

There are historical footnotes that ought to be mentioned in teaching about the Laodicean church and situation. Each note is given not as a history lesson, but as a way to highlight various phrases Christ speaks. Knowing Laodicea's historical situation helps us more pointedly understand the letter from Christ.

First, the Christian community in Laodicea held a connection to the church in Colossae located eleven miles away. The Laodicean church isn't mentioned in Acts or the epistles, save a few mentions in Paul's letter to the Colossian church. But what Paul does mention of the Laodicean church in Colossians is telling.

For instance, he tells the Colossians to "give my greetings to the brothers at Laodicea. . . . And when this letter has been read among you, have it also read in the church of the Laodiceans; and see that you also read the letter from Laodicea" (Colossians 4:15–16). So the Laodiceans were to read Colossians, but the Colossians were to read a letter Paul wrote the Laodiceans. This letter is lost to history, for not every word Paul taught—whether verbal or written—was the Word of God. But Paul seemed to think the Laodiceans needed the message he wrote to the Colossians.

The Colossian message battled false teachers who pulled them away from Christ. He wrote to them, "See to it that no one takes you captive by philosophy or empty deceit, according to human tradition, according to the elemental spirits of the world, and not according to Christ" (Colossians 2:8). So the Colossians were being pulled away from Christ into philosophies and human traditions according to the spirit of the world. Paul felt the Laodiceans needed to hear this message. As we shall see, Christ spoke to this error in Laodicea.

Second, Laodicea was a proud financial center. Laodicea housed a large Jewish community. They were wealthy, for history tells us they sent a substantial annual contribution to their brethren in Jerusalem. This grand gesture helps us understand the wealth of Laodicea.

Additionally, we know this city experienced two decimating earthquakes in the first century. In AD 17, they rebuilt the city with the financial aid of the Roman Empire, but in AD 60, they declined Rome's financial support. They were able to do so because of their enormous wealth. So this city was a wealthy one, and this impacted the church there.

Third, Laodicea was a proud clothing manufacturer. It might sound strange to our modern ears, but they were known as an exporter of a specialized black wool sheared from local flocks. They had become known for this rare material. Christ will allude to these black garments when He counsels them to purchase white garments from Him.

Fourth, Laodicea was a proud medical city. Famous local physicians were found on their city's coinage. A well-known medical school connected to the temple of Asclepius was relocated to Laodicea. Specifically, they had become famous for a medicinal eye and ear salve, which Christ would allude to.

So the Laodicean church lived in a wealthy town that placed a high value on fashion and physical health. They would have heard teachings designed to pull them away from the simplicity of Christ. The claim was that there is something better, bigger, stronger, healthier, and deeper than Christ. All of this contributed to their lukewarmness—not that it had to.

Description of Jesus

> And to the angel of the church in Laodicea write: "The words of the Amen, the faithful and true witness, the beginning of God's creation." (Revelation 3:14)

Christ's self-description gives us the first principle of protection against lukewarmness. Lukewarmness is remedied with a renewed and elevated view of Christ, so Christ gives them that elevated view afresh. Our view of Christ has a connection to our spiritual temperature. If we sense a need for our temperature to rise, to become hot toward Christ again, we need to see the gloriousness of Christ again. Notice how Jesus describes His glory for them.

"The words of the Amen. . ."

Here, Christ takes a title no mere man could dare touch. He is the Amen. He is the "so be it." He is the ratification of all things. But what does this allude to?

Paul gives us insight in 2 Corinthians: "For all the promises of God find their Yes in him. That is why it is through him that we utter our Amen to God for his glory" (2 Corinthians 1:20). Everything a person can have from God is bound up in Christ. Without Him, nothing is ratified. Without Him, there is no "so be it." All God's promises are confirmed and affirmed in Him. Because of Jesus, I get forgiveness, redemption, righteousness, the Holy Spirit, and on and on. In short, without Him I have nothing—I am poor. But the Amen makes me spiritually wealthy. It is all wrapped up in Him.

"The faithful and true witness. . ." Here, Christ contrasts Himself with the witness of the Laodiceans. They had obscured the light;

their witness perverted who God is, for He is not uncaring and lukewarm. But Christ's witness is faithful and true. Only at Christ can we look to know exactly what God is like. Even the holiest of men mars God's image in some way, but not so with Christ. He is the faithful and true witness.

In the last hours before His cross, Jesus taught His disciples. As He shared with them on their way to Gethsemane, Philip said, "Lord, show us the Father, and it is enough for us" (John 14:8).

> Jesus replied, "Have I been with you so long, and you still do not know me, Philip? Whoever has seen me has seen the Father. How can you say, 'Show us the Father'?" (John 14:9).

Jesus is the faithful witness of who the Father is. When you see Jesus, you see the Father. This is echoed in Hebrews: "He is the radiance of the glory of God and the exact imprint of His nature" (Hebrews 1:3). Jesus Christ is the exact imprint of God; He radiates God's glory. When you see Jesus, you're seeing God.

"The beginning of God's creation..." Here is where the Colossian temptation comes into play. Here, Jesus announces Himself as the ruler, source, and origin of God's creation; this is what it means to be the beginning of God's creation.

To the Colossians, Paul writes, "He is the image of the invisible God, the firstborn of all creation" (Colossians 1:15). Being the "firstborn" has little to do with a timeline and everything to do with position. He is over creation. Paul continues with various truths about Christ, the firstborn of all creation. "By him all things were created . . . through him and for him" (Colossians 1:16). "He is before all things, and in him all things hold together" (Colossians 1:17). "He is the head of . . . the church"

(Colossians 1:18). "In him all the fullness of God was pleased to dwell" (Colossians 1:19). Each statement is carefully selected to give emphasis to the glorious magnitude of Christ. Why turn to elemental teachings when you have Christ?

So again, we conclude this first point, lukewarmness is remedied with a renewed and elevated view of Christ. Like the emerging sun after a long winter, the glory of Christ was meant to bring heat to the Laodicean heart that had been dulled. The only way for it to become on fire again, if it had ever been so, was through an enlarged view of Jesus.

Get back to Christ. Find yourself infatuated with Him afresh. He is the glorious God. All we have is wrapped up in Him. It is all for Him, through Him, and about Him. Let us not drift from this.

Correction

> I know your works: you are neither cold nor hot. Would that you were either cold or hot! So, because you are lukewarm, and neither hot nor cold, I will spit you out of my mouth. For you say, I am rich, I have prospered, and I need nothing, not realizing that you are wretched, pitiable, poor, blind, and naked. (Revelation 3:15–17)

The honest word of Christ hit hard in Laodicea. As mentioned already, there was no word of commendation, no praise. His word, though tender in its source, was forceful in its truthfulness, and a hard truth it was. He saw their works and noticed they were "neither cold nor hot." He wished they were either cold or hot, but their lukewarmness tempted him to spit them out of his mouth. We will take these phrases piece by piece:

Lukewarm. The Laodicean would have had a unique understanding of this picture. Archaeologists have unearthed a five-mile-long aqueduct flowing from the Hierapolis to Laodicea. The water originated from a hot spring. So Laodicea drank mineral water that had turned from hot to lukewarm during the five-mile journey to their lips. This distasteful temperature was well known to the Laodiceans. They knew lukewarmness was in the middle of cold and hot.

Either cold or hot. Some have thought this a statement of two positives. A hot beverage is sometimes appropriate. So is a cold beverage. So perhaps Christ is saying they ought to be one or the other, and that either state is acceptable for the believer. I think, however, Christ is contrasting spiritual health (hot) with a rejection of Christ altogether (cold). Christ holds out the fervent believer or the hardened unbeliever. The gospel seems to demand either a hot or a cold response. In a sense, we might say lukewarmness is incompatible with the gospel. One should either be offended and incensed by it or blessed and rejoice over it. But the middle ground is not a proper response. Perhaps the "cold" Christ speaks of is closer to the state of preconverted Paul—harsh to the gospel but close to receiving it.

Spit them out. Jesus says he will spit them out of His mouth for this lukewarmness. Loss of salvation is not in view. He had walked among the seven golden lampstands. They were to bear the light of Christ to their world, but their lukewarmness was quenching the light. So, it seems, Christ is telling the Laodicean church they will lose their light-bearing essence if they continue in unrepentant lukewarmness.

But what is lukewarmness at its core? Again, it is playing the middle. A little heat, a little cold, mixed to form a middling temperature. Neither extreme—hot or cold—is reached. It isn't total indifference to Christ, but neither is it total fervency for Him. It's just the middle.

Perhaps an image from the sporting world would help. Imagine a great match or game between two impressive teams. Imagine a massive crowd. Then imagine them neither cheering or jeering but quietly sitting. No reaction whatsoever to the events playing out in front of them. This is lukewarmness. No care. No zeal. No passion. No fervency. The Lord hates it.

This definition of lukewarmness helps us find our second cure for it. If lukewarmness is playing the middle ground, then it is remedied by making a choice. "All in" is a modern phrase, and an escape from the tepid Christian state means coming to a place of decision. As Elijah said with power, "How long will you falter between two decisions?" (1 Kings 18:21). We must decide. Are we in—all in? Or are we out—all out? One way or the other, it is better than the lukewarm state. Again, the gospel does not allow room for the middle ground. If true, the gospel demands our all. If untrue, we should have nothing to do with it. The Laodicean church needed a decision.

Now, lukewarmness was only the symptom. There was a disease that led to lukewarmness. It hadn't been brought on by time or aging or familiarity. Here is why it came: "For you say, I am rich, I have prospered, and I need nothing, not realizing that you are wretched, pitiable, poor, blind, and naked." Here is where their tepid state originated—their inner attitude regarding themselves. They thought they were rich, prospering, and in need of nothing. There was no urgency, no need, no dependence upon God. They felt self-sufficient.

Here is where we see the Laodicean culture impacting the La-odicean church. The church had been discipled, but not by Christ.

They were disciples of Laodicea with all its wealth, all its love for bodily health, and all the outward trappings of luxury. The thorns and thistles had choked out the Word in the Laodicean church. They were stifled by the cares of this world. They thought their riches and goods satisfied their need. In reality, they had everything they wanted—but nothing they needed. Recall the church in Smyrna. They were suffering, poor, and persecuted, but Christ saw them as rich. This church is the opposite. They felt they had it all, but they had nothing.

This condition was lost on them. Jesus claimed they were "not realizing" the true state of things. The external trappings of the cosmos blinded them. They could not see their own wretchedness, poverty, and nakedness. This is where lukewarmness comes from—a serious lack of desperation for God. Jesus says, "Blessed are the poor in spirit" (Matthew 5:3). These are His first words in the Sermon on the Mount. This is His description of His kingdom, His people. Entrance into this kingdom begins with a sense of poverty within, a sense brought on by an encounter with the God of the universe. In comparison with His power and majesty, we sense our inadequacy. But the church in Laodicea didn't possess this realization. They were blind. So their lukewarmness was brought on by an incorrect view of the self.

Solution

> I counsel you to buy from me gold refined by fire, so that you may be rich, and white garments so that you may clothe yourself and the shame of your nakedness may not be seen, and salve to anoint your eyes, so that you may see. Those whom I love, I reprove and discipline, so be zealous and repent. Behold, I stand at the door and knock. If anyone hears my voice and opens

the door, I will come in to him and eat with him, and
he with me. (Revelation 3:18–20)

Christ gave them counsel. The history of Laodicea comes rushing
into our minds as we read it. They were wealthy—gold abounded—but they were to buy gold refined by fire from Christ. They
were exporters of black garments, but to cover shame, they were
to buy white garments from Christ. They produced a medicinal
eye salve, but they were to buy eye salve from Christ to get spiritual sight.

All of this speaks of something truer. There's wealth; then
there's truer wealth. There's clothing; then there's truer clothing.
There's medicine; then there's truer medicine. Christ provides
that which is the truest. They were to dispense with that which
didn't matter in order to get from Christ the riches, clothing, and
medicine that mattered. Set your mind on this:

The true gold. As long as the believer thinks of money incorrectly, he will be in bondage. It is an instrument, a tool. We aren't
to be reigned by it. It is not our chief end. We cannot trust it, because it gives no true security and no true joy. There is no satisfaction when we see wealth incorrectly. But Christ pleaded with
this church to get the real riches. Again, remember Smyrna. In
their pain and persecution, they had the real wealth. They knew
life was about more than possessions. They gained better possessions when they gained fellowship with Christ, prayer, and
fruitfulness.

The true clothing. Christ had no literal white garments for them;
this is figurative. The black garments produced in Laodicea were
not the problem, but what these garments produced in the people
was. This is not hard to imagine. Even today clothing is meant to
give definition, style, and confidence. Clothes are designed to say

something about you, and certain clothes make you feel a certain way. To feel confident, many people need to look a certain way. Dressing inappropriately for an occasion makes us shy or bashful. But Christ asks us to get something else for our confidence and acceptance—not the outward, but the inward. He covers shame with His clothing. Too often man looks to the external to generate a feeling of acceptance or worthiness, but this is best found from Christ. Covered by His blood, clothed with His white garments, we are more loved and accepted than we could ever know. This love is a better giver of confidence and acceptance than any weight loss program or new wardrobe could ever provide.

The true medicine. Again, they had loved medicine, advancements in health, in Laodicea. Their doctors were their heroes, and science was their savior. But where science could help the body a little, it couldn't help the soul at all. For that, Christ was needed. This church had fallen in love with health that is external, but Christ offered internal medicine. He could give them true spiritual sight.

In all three of these, we learn a valuable lesson in combatting lukewarmness. The whole value system of this church had to change, and lukewarmness is remedied by reevaluating your value system. They had to see that Christ had more for them, and we must see He has more for us. The way up is down. His real wealth, His real garments, and His real medicine all await us. We are to approach Him, to get them from Him. His gospel turned the world upside down, and it turns our values upside down as well. He loves not what we love, but something better. He longs to give this view of life to us as well.

Finally, we come to the last tool to combat lukewarmness. It is simple. Lukewarmness is remedied through personal interaction with Christ. The picture is stirring, if not heartbreaking. Jesus stands at the door . . . knocking. The One with the keys to open doors no man can shut will not force this door. This door can only be opened from the inside. He knocks. He longs to enter. But the resident must open the door.

This closed door is a clear picture of the Laodicean church. Christ wanted personal interaction with them, but they had to want it in return, and to want it meant to open the door.

This desire for personal interaction has forever been the heart of God. He has always wanted personal interaction with humanity. Eden shows us this. God walked in the garden in the cool of the day looking for His people (Genesis 3:8). But it isn't only in Eden where we see this from God. He walked with Enoch (Genesis 5:24). He walked with Noah (Genesis 6:9). He instituted a sacrificial system complete with a fellowship offering, a meal of sorts man could share with God. Christ came and He dined, sitting with humanity. He was relational to His core. This is God. He longs for personal interaction with man. In this era, He resides within His people; He could not be closer.

But the Laodicean church had kept fellowship with Christ at arm's length. Christ knocked at the door. Would they open? Will you? The tepid heart is healed through real spiritual experiences with Christ—an enjoyment of His presence and fellowship. Churches everywhere preach the importance of getting into His Word and praying, and this is preached for a good reason. His Word and His invitation to prayer are sacred grounds where He engages in fellowship with us. Some have attempted to create other pathways to Him, but if the path isn't found in Scripture, it ought to be rejected. Christ is found in His Word. He is found in prayer. He is found in the fast. He is found in worship. He is found in service. He is found with His people. Open the door and interact with Him.

Promise

> The one who conquers, I will grant him to sit with me
> on my throne, as I also conquered and sat down with
> my Father on his throne. (Revelation 3:21)

As with all the promises to the overcomer in all the letters, this promise is eternal in nature. Christ sits on the throne with His Father. We will sit with Him on His throne. Ultimate victory and dominion are ours with and in Christ. Because He overcame, we overcome. "Who is it that overcomes the world except the one who believes that Jesus is the Son of God?" (1 John 5:5). We will sit as overcomers forever with Christ.

Again, for the last time, we are told to hear what the Spirit says to the churches. Listen. Hear Him. He seems to say that lukewarmness has no compatibility with the gospel. The cross of Christ demands an extreme reaction in one direction or another. Don't fall prey to the trap of self-sufficiency, but see the all-sufficiency of Christ. He is worthy of our adoration. He is the Amen, the faithful and true witness, the firstborn over all creation. There is no one like Him. Open the door to Him and enjoy fellowship with His greatness. When you do, your lukewarmness will dissolve, and soon, you will find yourself engulfed in the flames of passion for Christ.

> He who has an ear, let him hear what the Spirit says to
> the churches. (Revelation 3:22)

CHAPTER 9

The Good Shepherd

Who walks among the seven golden lampstands.
(Revelation 2:1)

Christ is presented as the Good Shepherd. In this role, He guides, protects, and disciplines His sheep, but all of it is done with the best interest of His sheep in mind. The still waters, the green pastures, the tablelands: all of it for the sheep. Even the journey through the valley of the shadow of death is a necessary path for His sheep. That path takes us to the beautiful places the Shepherd has in store.

This Psalm 23 perspective is how we ought to see the seven letters of Christ to the churches of Asia Minor. At times they are encouraging. At other times they are confrontational. Sometimes they are corrective, and sometimes affirming. The Shepherd knew what each church needed from Him. With His rod and staff and sling, He went to work.

Christ still works for His sheep today. In this final chapter, we will quickly return to each church. We will note their main issue or quality and apply Christ's exhortations to our hearts. For each church, I will provide a biblical character or story that embodies the message to that church. Allow the Spirit to interact with your heart. Where are you today? Which letter is yours? Or how many of them are yours? As we allow Christ to shepherd us, we are led to the green pastures . . . but we must allow Him that opportunity.

Ephesus—The Cold Church (Revelation 2:4–5)

> But I have this against you, that you have abandoned the love you had at first. Remember therefore from where you have fallen; repent, and do the works you did at first. If not, I will come to you and remove your lampstand from its place, unless you repent. (Revelation 2:4–5)

Ephesus was praised by Christ, mostly for their solid doctrinal positions and tireless work for His kingdom. Still, their issue was serious. They had abandoned the love they had at first. They were meant to grow in a response love to the powerful love of Christ. Their work and toil had begun to disconnect from the cross, the love of Christ. They were going through the motions of ministry work but were not fueled by the love of Christ. Christ urged them to return to that early love, a love of simple response to His great love for them.

One day the prophet Elisha was called to a building site. The school of the prophets was expanding, which was good, but a borrowed ax head had fallen into the river, which was bad. The young prophet who lost control of the ax was upset. The ax head was deep in that rushing water, lost to the river. He alerted Elisha, who asked him where it fell in. After discerning the spot, Elisha cut off a stick of wood and threw it at that spot. The iron ax head began to float, so he reached out and recovered it.

If you have left your first love, you must go back to the spot you lost it. Repent, return, go back. Remember the wood of the cross and begin to rejoice afresh at what Christ has done for you. Remember Peter. He had gotten an exalted view of himself during Christ's ministry, which climaxed in his declaration that he'd never deny Christ. Of course, he did deny Christ—three times, and embarrassingly so. He wept bitterly over his failure. But Christ later met Peter on the shores of Galilee. Around the early morning fire, Jesus asked Peter, "Do you love me more than these?" Three times he asked the question, just as Peter had denied Jesus three times. This was restoration. Jesus took Peter back to His first love; a love for Christ, not a love for fruitfulness. Let Him take you there if He must.

Smyrna—The Hated Church (Revelation 2:9–10)

> I know your tribulation and your poverty (but you are rich) and the slander of those who say that they are Jews and are not, but are a synagogue of Satan. Do not fear what you are about to suffer. Behold, the devil is about to throw some of you into prison, that you may be tested, and for ten days you will have tribulation. Be faithful unto death, and I will give you the crown of life. (Revelation 2:9–10)

Smyrna experienced the fellowship of the sufferings of Christ. They had tribulation and poverty, and they were slandered. Persecution was their lot. Christ encouraged them with His knowledge of their suffering. He knew of their persecution not only because He saw it, but also because He'd lived it. Everything they endured had first been endured by their Lord.

Imagine the man Noah. He had found grace in the eyes of the Lord during a time when the thoughts of all of humanity were perpetually evil. Good had been suppressed by evil, but Noah found God's kindness. The story is famous. Noah was told to build an ark by God, a transport of protection from the coming doom of a worldwide flood. This was long obedience; it took years to complete that structure, but "he did all that God commanded him" (see Genesis 6:22, 7:5, 16). In the face of laughter and the taunts of man, Noah built. The church in Smyrna endured in the same way. Hated, they built. Persecuted, they endured.

Christ told them not to fear all they would suffer. The exhortation is ominous, for it promised no escape from the suffering; instead, it told of Christ's help through the suffering. Perhaps they (and we) would be helped to remember the initial waves of persecution that hit the early believers. Saul held the coats of the religious leaders who reigned stones down upon Stephen the deacon. This unleashed a persecution that had been quietly coming to a boil. But during the ensuing wave of violence, the church endured and the gospel spread. As they ran, they preached, and what the enemy meant for evil, God used for good. This is powerful! Perhaps you are being hated, in one way or another, for your love for Christ and His gospel. Embrace the reality that Christ can use that evil for great good. He might use it to kill your need for the praise of man. He might use it to bring the persecutor to a place of decision for Christ. He might use it to spread the gospel. He might use it to purify His church. But He can use it. Do not fear what you are about to suffer.

Pergamum—The Deceived Church (Revelation 2:14–16)

> But I have a few things against you: you have some there who hold the teaching of Balaam, who taught Balak to put a stumbling block before the sons of Israel, so that they might eat food sacrificed to idols and practice sexual immorality. So also you have some who hold the

teaching of the Nicolaitans. Therefore repent. If not, I
will come to you soon and war against them with the
sword of my mouth. (Revelation 2:14–16)

The Pergamum church was loved by Christ, but they had invited
cancer into their midst. The cancer was doctrinal, named as the
teaching of Balaam and the Nicolaitans by Christ. But this doctrine seems to be brought on by a desire. They embraced these
errors, "so that they might eat food sacrificed to idols and practice sexual immorality." For these believers, their hearts led them
to a doctrine. Bad doctrine can begin in the mind, of course, but
not in Pergamum. There, it began in the heart . . . in the feelings
. . . in the realm of desire.

Are we not in danger of following our feelings more than God's
word? Believers claim Scripture to be authoritative, but it must
be functionally so. It must have real—not just perceived or po-
sitional—authority. God knew this was a danger to Israel. He
warned them not to follow their hearts (Numbers 15:39). This
was a real danger. His Word is an excellent North Star to navigate
the perilous storms of our emotions and desires. They turn and
shift, as is obvious by looking at the differing tendencies and perspectives in cultures around the globe. But the believer's beliefs
aren't to be shaped by culture, but by Christ and His Word. We
aren't disciples of our environment but of Christ.

When the teaching of Balaam was received, the people of Israel
were on their way out of Egypt. It was a perilous time. God had
promised that through Abraham—and subsequently Isaac and
Jacob—the whole world would be blessed. This was a promise
of the Christ, the Messiah. But for that promise to find fulfillment, they as a people had to be preserved. But Balaam taught
the Moabite king Balak to send in Moabite women to join to the
Israelite men. They engaged sexually—but they also engaged in

worshipping the Moabites' Baal. This was a deadly serious moment for Israel and for all of humanity. The cross was in jeopardy. A man name Phinehas saw the plague of God unleashed upon the people. Thousands died before Phinehas saw a man brazenly persist in the sin. He executed the man because he was jealous for God and His glory. His act stopped the wrath of God, saving Israel. God praised him for his jealousy for God.

Perhaps this jealous attitude from Phinehas will help the believer tempted to go the route of Pergamum. We aren't Israel, so we won't respond in the same way Phinehas did, but the same jealousy can fill our hearts. Long for the full allegiance of God's people to Him.

Thyatira—The Mixed Church (Revelation 2:20)

> But I have this against you, that you tolerate that woman Jezebel, who calls herself a prophetess and is teaching and seducing my servants to practice sexual immorality and to eat food sacrificed to idols. (Revelation 2:20)

The Thyatiran church was being destroyed from the inside out. Some had received the teaching of Jezebel, likely a reference to the Old Testament woman with the same name. The original Jezebel sought to kill the worship of Yahweh by adding the worship of Baal. She knew the worship of Baal would eventually suffocate the worship of God. The Jezebel of Thyatira called herself a prophetess and claimed to offer the deep things of God, but Christ called them "the deep things of Satan." This is an old tactic of the enemy. We like to say, "If you can't beat them, join them," but Satan loves to reverse the statement. His tactic goes, "If you can't join them, beat them." Apostasy first, then persecution next.

The enemy always attempts to add to the simplicity of Christ. Politics, career, wealth, status, sin—whatever he can add that will kill the worship of God is fine with him. The goal is simple: suffocate devotion to God with devotion to other things. The third soil of Christ's parable of the sower comes to mind (Mark 4:18–19). The seed grew but was choked out by the weeds. Christ said they were the cares of this world and the deceitfulness of riches. Christ looks for—and deserves—full devotion and allegiance. Man cannot serve two masters. But Thyatira was mixed, and that mixture was killing them.

Hosea served God in such a time. God said the land committed "great whoredom by forsaking the Lord" (Hosea 1:2). God instructed Hosea to marry a woman, Gomer, who would abandon him in favor of a life of prostitution. She gave herself to other lovers. Their marriage served as an illustration of God's marriage to Israel. They had departed, joining themselves to other lovers. The Thyatiran tendency does likewise. But we are called to hear the cry of the Spirit, to return to our Husband, to become singly devoted to Christ. This church was losing their life; they needed to turn to Christ for the deep things of life. The deep things weren't found in idols, careers, wealth, family, politics, or any other pursuit. The deep things are in Christ alone.

Sardis—The Dead Church (Revelation 3:1–2)

> And to the angel of the church in Sardis write: "The words of him who has the seven spirits of God and the seven stars. I know your works. You have the reputation of being alive, but you are dead. Wake up, and strengthen what remains and is about to die, for I have not found your works complete in the sight of my God." (Revelation 3:1–2)

The church in Sardis looked alive as far as humans could tell. That was their reputation. They weren't an obviously dead church, but Christ saw them as such. "You have the reputation of being alive, but you are dead." Their city had twice been defeated through sleep, and now the same was occurring within the church. They were the walking dead. Only Christ could say such a thing. The assessment of Christ was not a death sentence, however. He is the resurrected King, and He is able to resurrect.

He told this church to wake up and strengthen what remained. They had the outward form of the church, and that needed no changing, but the inner reality needed to match the outward form. To wake up and let the resurrection power of Christ breathe life into their actions was their necessity.

David, a man after God's heart, extolled his son to serve God with a whole heart and a willing mind (1 Chronicles 28:9). Solomon began well, but eventually his many wives "turned away his heart" from God (1 Kings 11:3). He did not serve God with his whole heart. This was what led to the death of the church in Sardis. The heart was gone, lost, and dead.

In the earthly ministry of Christ, there was a day on the north coast of Galilee. He came to the shore, and messengers awaited. Jairus, who ruled the local synagogue, had a twelve-year-old daughter. She was sick, lying at the point of death. Jesus agreed to see her. The hope was that He would heal her. The journey to the girl was interrupted, however, by a woman with a hidden sickness. She touched Jesus's robe, for she privately told herself, "If I touch the hem of his garment I will be healed." Jesus paused until she confessed to being the one who touched Him. Power was released from Christ. She was healed. He knew it. The scene was beautiful, but then it turned ugly again when messengers returned. "Do not trouble the teacher any further, for the girl has died." Hope was lost. Healing would not come.

But Jesus replies by saying, "She is not dead, but sleeping" (Luke 8:52). Only Christ can say this. To every human observer, the girl was dead. They laughed at Jesus for the saying. But His perspective is different. What is death to us is sleep to Him, for He can raise, and raise He did. The same is true for the church in Sardis and any dead believer. It is death, but Christ sees sleep, for He can resurrect you. Wake up. Let Him breathe His life into you afresh.

Philadelphia—The Open-Door Church (Revelation 3:7–8)

> And to the angel of the church in Philadelphia write: "The words of the holy one, the true one, who has the key of David, who opens and no one will shut, who shuts and no one opens. I know your works. Behold, I have set before you an open door, which no one is able to shut. I know that you have but little power, and yet you have kept my word and have not denied my name." (Revelation 3:7–8)

Philadelphia, like Smyrna, had no rebuke from Christ. But unlike Smyrna, they were not an overly persecuted group. No, they had an opportunity from Christ. He portrayed Himself as the One who opens and closes doors, and He had opened a door for the church in Philadelphia. Part of the purpose of the city of Philadelphia was to carry the Greco-Roman culture to the regions beyond. But the church was to carry the gospel to the regions beyond. No longer missionaries of culture, they were now missionaries for Christ. Paul told the church that we are ambassadors for Christ (2 Corinthians 5:20); the church in Philadelphia had this opportunity.

Their strength was small, but it was enough for Christ. He would aid them, and in their weakness, He would be strong.

When Paul and Barnabas were on their first missionary journey, they came to Derbe and Lystra. There, rejection grew strong. Paul was stoned to the point where everyone assumed him dead. He eventually rose up and went back into the city, preaching, before they departed. On a later journey, Paul passed through the same region. There again, he found a young believer named Timothy. He saw something in him, so he invited him to join his missionary work. The assumption is that Timothy had given his life to Christ during Paul's first journey through town. He was familiar with the pain and suffering of the Christian worker. He'd become a believer from that backdrop. So when Timothy accepted Paul's call, it did not come from a Pollyannaish view of missionary work. He knew the rowing would be hard. Still, he went. He continued on to Thessalonica, Corinth, Ephesus, Philippi—anywhere Paul asked him to go. In other words, Timothy said yes. Because he went through one open door, new doors opened. This is the spirit the Philadelphian church needed—a willingness to go, to say yes to Christ and His opportunity.

Laodicea—The Lukewarm Church (Revelation 3:15–17)

> I know your works: you are neither cold nor hot. Would that you were either cold or hot! So, because you are lukewarm, and neither hot nor cold, I will spit you out of my mouth. For you say, I am rich, I have prospered, and I need nothing, not realizing that you are wretched, pitiable, poor, blind, and naked. (Revelation 3:15–17).

The Laodicean church had fallen, like their water supply, into lukewarmness. It was the saddest of states to Christ. He would spit them out of His mouth; they would lose their illuminative power. No light came from them because of this lack of heat. They needed to become fired up for Christ again. This would come through a renewed high view of Christ. He is the Amen all the church's promises are wrapped up in. He is the faithful and true witness who accurately expresses God to us. He is the firstborn of all creation in whom we find all our meaning. This lukewarmness would also be defeated through choosing fully for or against Christ by seeing their deep need for Him. The door of fellowship with Christ had to be opened. If it was, the lukewarmness would dissipate, giving way to heat again.

The days judges ruled over pockets of Israel were dark days: "In those days there was no king in Israel. Everyone did what was right in his own eyes" (Judges 21:25). But in the days of the judges, there were still bright spots of hot devotion to Christ. Ruth, a Moabite convert, stood out so beautifully as such that an entire Bible book is devoted to her story. The days were so dark the story of light had to be told. In days of darkness, days where lukewarmness in the church runs strong, believers must know there is another way. The Ruth spirit still exists. We do not have to get swept up in a callousness toward Christ. Tepidness can give way to fire. Go to Him for the true wealth, the true garments, the true medicine. He works in us if we will allow Him access. Reject the Pharisaical spirit of self-approval. Replace it with the mood of the tax collector who clung to the possibility of God's grace and mercy (see Luke 18:9–14).

> He who has an ear, let him hear what the Spirit says to the churches. (Revelation 3:22)

Bibliography

Aune, David E. Revelation 1–5. Vol. 52A, *Word Biblical Commentary*. Dallas: Word, Incorporated, 1998.

Barker, Kenneth L. *Expositor's Bible Commentary*, Abridged Edition: New Testament. Grand Rapids, MI: Zondervan Publishing House, 1994.

Bruce, F. F. *New International Bible Commentary*. Grand Rapids, MI: Zondervan Publishing House, 1979.

Henry, Matthew. *Matthew Henry's Commentary on the Whole Bible: Complete and Unabridged in One Volume*. Peabody, MA: Hendrickson, 1994.

Jamieson, Robert, A. R. Fausset, and David Brown. *Commentary Critical and Explanatory on the Whole Bible*. Oak Harbor, WA: Logos Research Systems, Inc., 1997.

Keener, Craig S. *The IVP Bible Background Commentary: New Testament*. Downers Grove, IL: InterVarsity Press, 1993.

Morgan, G. Campbell. *The Letters of Our Lord*. Old Tappan, NJ: Fleming G. Revell, 1975.

Mounce, Robert H. *The Book of Revelation: The New International Commentary on the New Testament*. Grand Rapids, MI: William B. Eerdmans, 1977.

Walvoord, John F. *The Revelation of Jesus Christ: A Commentary.* Chicago: Moody Press, 1989.

Walvoord, John F., and Roy B. Zuck, eds. *The Bible Knowledge Commentary: An Exposition of the Scriptures.* Wheaton, IL: Victor Books, 1985.

About the Author

Nate Holdridge has served as pastor of Calvary Monterey Church in Monterey, California, since 2008. Calvary's vision is to see Jesus famous, and Nate teaches and writes with that aim at nateholdridge.com.

Let Us Hear